DRAW YOUR STRENGTH
FROM THE LORD

- The Author of this book has written four others to confirm the faith of millions who are sorely tempted to doubt in this age of confusion.

- Now he wants these people to "confirm their brethren" and share their convictions with others.

- Here he describes how this can be done: not by fragile human means but by un-limited divine assistance which is available to everyone.

- Catch a little of the Author's zeal — and then see to it that the flame spreads!

Father Pads Reynolds O.S.B

Imprimi potest
+ Eugene Medved, O.S.B.
Abbot,
Westminster Abbey,
Mission, B.C.
March, 1976

Nihil Obstat
Daniel Carey
Censor Librorum

Imprimatur
James F. Carney, D.D.
Archbishop of Vancouver
March 1, 1976

Library of Congress Card Number: 76-7102
ISBN 0 - 8189 – 1133 – 6

© Copyright 1976 by
ALBA HOUSE COMMUNICATIONS
Canfield, Ohio, 44406

Printed in the United States of America

DRAW YOUR STRENGTH FROM THE LORD

TO OUR LADY –
MOTHER OF GOOD COUNSEL
FOR EVERY MENDER

FOREWORD

The writing of this book has suggested itself as a sequel to my other four books which, one might say, form a team to be met in sequence and which are intended to invite the reader to enter into a far larger team of *Menders* inspired by God to fight the damage being done by Satan in the Church and in the world.

The Captain of this team is my life story, *A REBEL FROM RICHES*. I hope it will make readers my close friends. The second, *HOW COME MY FAITH?* suggests a sound foundation for Christian living. The third, *PROJECT SAINTHOOD YOUR BUSINESS*, puts *HOW COME* into action. And number four, *LET'S MEND THE MESS!* should serve as the "tackle" member of the team to enlist the support of an army of *Menders* engaged in *Project Sainthood*.

Not long ago, a friend of mine was scanning the paperbacks in a Catholic book store and asked the clerk if he could see some of Father Bede Reynolds' books. The lady said: "We had some, but I don't think we have any more. Most of our sales now are *contemporary* books." One wonders if it is the readers or the feeders that have brought about this definition. Should it be said that a book published in 1976 that defends the Catholic Church that came from Christ to the Apostles and faces the world fortified by the Second Vatican Council, is "old hat" before it is printed?

Apparently the books which readers are encouraged to seek, are those which have done their best to prove that moral restraint is no longer consistent with the findings of science. If that is true, may we not say that the call – *Let's Mend The Mess!* is over-due and try to reinforce it now with *DRAW YOUR STRENGTH FROM THE LORD!*

CONTENTS

CHAPTER I

HE IS VERY
CLOSE TO YOU

Those readers who are familiar with my writing may know almost word for word what to expect from me as we start this my last book. But this time I am going to fool you just a little. I am not going to begin this Retreat by another elaboration of the theme which is expressed by the phrase of the Lord's Prayer: "Thy Will Be Done."

Of course, what I am aiming at is just another way of saying the same thing. But I want to put it in another way to emphasize what might otherwise seem to be expecting too much from those of my readers who are "living in the world" and still are trying to fulfill to the best of their ability the purpose of their existence.

And the idea is this: The full understanding of our Faith should inspire every Christian to see that the only way of life which really fits with the Light of Christ's teaching is *The Way of Perfection*, seeking the counsels of perfection, not just the precept to keep out of jail and hope for a state of grace at the hour of death. And here is the important point for us, here and now: While the State of Perfection might be called the professional goal of those who are called to be priests and religious, it is no less available to those whose status in the world prevents the realization of a religious vocation.

The way of perfection, then, that I am recommending is no less than the way of life leading to sainthood, as contrasted with the way of life which only hopes against hope of being reconciled to God at the hour of death. The only incentive to the latter course is the notion that worldly motives, worldly comforts, worldly consolations, worldly success, have real standing in comparison with spiritual success; that these things have value that justifies their pursuit even when their pursuit departs from the way of perfection.

Perhaps you are thinking: "No, Father, it isn't that we set store by these worldly motives. We can see that a better knowledge of our Faith should make it more and more clear that nothing is more to be desired than sainthood. But we simply have to face the facts and recognize our frailty. Since the Fall of Man we are victims of the temptations permitted by God and we cannot expect to be saints just because we admit that, in the abstract, sin does not make sense, and worldly success is vain."

And that is just exactly the response that I wanted to trick you into making! Make no mistake. The canonized saints are just as frail as any of you. So are the canonized saints exposed to temptations, just as any of you are. BUT the difference between their approach and the approach of this response which I have suggested, or the response of any compromise with conscience, is that saints have taken seriously the admonition of Christ: "He who abides in Me and I in him, he it is who bears much fruit; because apart from Me you can produce nothing." (John 15:5). That is Christ's promise that those who *do* cooperate with grace *can* do what it takes to be saints; not by their own power, but by the power of God. And, as Saint Paul advises the Ephesians: "Draw your strength from the Lord; from that mastery which His power supplies." (6:10).

So, what I hope to do is to clear away the false notion that anyone can set out to be a saint on his own, and the equally false notion that anyone is in a position where it would be impossible for him to become a saint, if he or she makes use of the help that Christ will give. And, with that as a basis, I want to recommend, not just a study of our Faith with an eye to improvement, but a study of the Way of Perfection with an eye to sanctification.

And I want to assure you that there is no one who is in-eligible to pursue this course with profit. Not only with profit, but with such tremendous profit that it may frighten you to recall that you have heretofore had any hesitation about starting. Furthermore, there are no situations which necessitate or admit of delay.

Discouraging ill-success with problems of married life; discouraging ill-success in finding a solution to financial or business problems; discouraging ill-success in meeting various kinds of temptations; discouraging ill-success in guiding children or in dealing with any of our family or associates; discouraging ill-success in bridling our own impulses to say or do things we are afterwards sorry for; discouraging ill-success in obtaining a goal or objective of any kind — None of these make one ineligible to start today toward sainthood by the Way of Perfection. In fact, problems and trials can be turned into assets, as very many of the saints have often proved.

The crux of the whole situation rests upon the development of our capacity for union with Christ in Faith and Hope and Love and (now comes by theme-song) and Will. Abandonment to the will of Christ *is* the Way of Perfection. It is the key which supernaturalizes every act of ours and obtains for us the power of Christ to enable us to "bear much fruit" and, incidentally, to find peace and joy in life, even when surrounded by the most unhappy trials and problems.

Let me hasten to remove any possibility of disillusionment in offering the prospect of peace and joy to accompany the disciple in the Way of Perfection. There is no guarantee that problems and trials will disappear. In fact, their increase may be a good indication of the approval of our Master and Teacher.

"Those whom I love, I rebuke and chastise; be fervent therefore and repent. Behold, I stand at the door and knock. If any one hears My voice and opens the door, I will come in to him and sup with him and he with Me. To him that shall overcome I will give to sit with Me upon My throne as

I also have overcome and am set down with My Father on His throne." (Apoc. 3:19-21).

There is the offer! No matter what trials may prevail, Christ will come in and unite His strength with our weakness if we will but open the door and unite our will with His.

The will NOT to believe that this is true is the only unforgivable sin. Such a will is resistance against the prompting of the Holy Spirit. It desupernaturalizes our motive and leaves us without Christ, to fight our battle alone. "Without Me you can do nothing." But with the help that He promises to those who sup with Him, sainthood can emerge from every vicissitude of life.

And one thing more: The Way of Perfection and sainthood for those in the world does not necessarily involve the counsel to: "Go, sell all that thou hast and give to the poor." (Matt. 19:21). One can be detached from the world and still live in it. It is true that there are degrees of perfection and perhaps the highest state, and one which is well worth all it costs, is the goal of those who go the limit. But perfection leading to sainthood is by no means barred to those who live in the world and follow the holy vocation of lay Christian life, either in the married state or single.

Now, there are various ways of approaching the Way of Perfection. But, as I have said, it is my conviction that the most fundamental and sure-fire approach is through a full understanding of our Faith and all the objective truth involved in the promises of Christ. I do not mean by this that I propose to guide you to the Way of Perfection by giving you a course in Apologetics or even a course in Christian Doctrine. That might be useful, but I wish to aim higher than that. I wish to ask you not to be frightened if I designate our approach to the Way of Perfection as a study of Ascetical Theology. That merely means that we will study what God has done and still does for us, as the most efficacious motive of true devotion.

There are innumerable books on spirituality designed primarily to edify the reader. One of the best of the classics of this type is Saint Francis de Sales' "*Treatise on the Love of God*". As we study together the Way of Perfection, I wish to try to follow a course which will instruct as well as edify and promote devotion. To do this, I propose to follow the path marked out for the Spiritual Life by Father Adolphe Tanquerey. This is based on the principle that knowledge leads to devotion and perfection.

The first fruit of knowledge, however, should be an appreciation of the intimate relationship between each and every soul in a state of Grace and Jesus Christ, the omnipotent God in heaven and the loving indwelling principle of the supernatural life within us. It takes time to learn and to realize this intimacy in its full magnificence. And a lot of valuable time would be lost in making progress toward perfection if we had to wait for full knowledge of the truth in order to profit by its effects. So I want to ask you to take this on faith at once and try to learn to advert to it almost constantly and in every detail of your life.

The truth is this: Christ, who is the Incarnate representative of the Holy Trinity, is as intimately present to you at every moment of your life, with His infinite love, His infinite wisdom and His infinite power, available for your welfare, as if you were the only soul ever created. This is true whether you are experiencing the greatest ecstacies of spiritual fervor, or are experiencing the most painful trials of your lifetime.

It is not possible for us to find an analogy in human experience for the intimacy of this presence and its consequences. Various attempts are made by comparing it to the availability of the light of the same sun for all, or the equal benefit of air to breathe for all. But these fall far short of reality because the intimacy of God's presence is essentially a divine property. Any finite example simply pictures the sharing of a part of a large supply, whereas God's presence is whole and entire and infinite and without parts, equally present for all.

It is impossible for us to know HOW God can be devoting His attention, as it were, exclusively to us and at the same time equally attentive to and present to the billions of other souls who occupy the world with us. That is why we have to take it on faith THAT God can do what He tells us He will do.

Each one can, perhaps, be helped to grasp this truth quickly, by looking back over his or her own life for evidence of its effect. And that may include the most harrowing experiences of our lives, even more definitely than the most pleasant ones. This notion is expressed by the former agnostic, Alfred Noyes, in the story of his conversion entitled: *THE UNKNOWN GOD*. He says: "There are few adults who if they look back through their lives and are honest with themselves, have not some knowledge of the directing and shaping influence of this real intimate presence of a divinity that 'shapes our ends, rough hew them how we will.' " (p. 306).

This has been so obvious in my own life that all anxiety for the future or perplexity in the present have practically vanished from my thoughts. They are replaced by a confidence that knows for certain that every detail that unfolds, day by day and hour by hour, is a part of the mosaic of my life that is composed by God with divine perfection. The result is a peace of soul and an enthusiasm for work which would be impossible in any purely human circumstances of life however consoling they might be.

In recent years, I am often amazed at the completeness of God's attention to my affairs even in small details. Whenever I am sent on a mission or whenever anything out of the ordinary occurs, I say to myself: "What has God in mind for me now?" And almost invariably I find the answer in subsequent events.

God's attention is, however, most obvious in the great events of one's life. And an interesting sidelight in that regard, in my own experiences, is that the two greatest evidences of God's loving interest in my welfare seemed, at the time of their occurrence, to be two of the most unwelcome circumstances of my life. The first was that the girl He gave me for a wife was a Catholic. The second was that He took her from me while in the prime of life. The first, by a miracle of grace, gave me the Catholic Faith. The second, by a miracle of grace, gave me the priesthood.

You may feel that you cannot see the pattern quite as clearly marked in your own life. If so, it may be partly because you have neglected to advert to the certainty that it comes from God, and so have failed to profit by that certainty. But I beg you to accept it as true and to make immediate use of it pending the confirmation of it by our further study.

Your reading of this book and your attention to this invitation of mine is the result of a chain of circumstances carefully planned and arranged by God for each one of you. It is a part of the mosaic of your life which is being assembled by God. The picture He is making is different for each one of you. He is inviting you now to have a share in making the finish of the picture the most beautiful part of it. He is inviting you to cooperate with the Artist instead of coasting along with indifference or inattention to the most important phase of your life, namely; the development of spiritual perfection, the quest for sainthood.

And this is true regardless of whether I am successful in making the quest seem interesting and exciting. The fruit of your participation in this project will be entirely a product of the intimacy between yourself and God. It will function all the time during the seven hundred twenty hours of each month, not just during the seven or eight hours that you will spend reading these pages.

Specifically, it will slip into our mind whenever an annoying situation arises and will enable you to make the outcome less unfortunate than it would have been if you had not adverted to God's presence and His offer of help. It will also come to your rescue if and when there may be temptations to be less good, less charitable, less loving, less dutiful toward your work and your neighbor, than you would have been if it were not for God's immediate presence and offer to help you.

It will come into your mind, whenever you say your prayers, that you are talking with someone who is your best and gentlest friend who is able to do all that is necessary about your every need. It will also make those prayers more concerned with cooperating with your Friend's will than

with trying to bend His will to yours. It will make you toy
with the idea of sampling the blessing of Mass and the Sacraments during the week and not just on Sunday or even rele-
gated to Saturday evening.

Above all, it will give you peace of soul in submissive acceptance of all that happens as being part of the loving will
of God. It will invite you to pray as the Church prays in so
many of the Masses of Ordinary Time, for example, the
opening prayer of the Sixth Sunday:

> **"God our Father, You have promised to remain for ever
> with those who do what is just and right. Help us to live
> in your presence."**

The Way of Perfection upon which we hope to travel
leads inevitably to sainthood IF it is built upon cooperation
with the will of Christ who is present in our hearts and
aware of everything we do. It does not aim at spiritual or
temporal consolation and cares little for ease and pleasure in
wordly pursuits, but finds joy in whatever Christ provides.

If we succeed in clinching this notion of Christ's intimate
presence in our affairs, we will be ready to gain the greatest
harvest as we proceed with Father Tanquerey who assures us
in his preface that: "A vivid realization of the truths of faith
is the strongest incentive toward correction of faults and
practice of virtues." (p. vii).

And so, Beloved: "Draw your strength from the Lord,
from that mastery which His power supplies." (Eph. 6:10).

CHAPTER II

IN THE BEGINNING

In our opening chapter of this DRAW YOUR STRENGTH FROM THE LORD, we discussed the utility, the practicality and the desirability of making the pursuit of Christian Perfection the predominant guiding principle of our lives. It was suggested that you might save time and hasten your progress in the Way of Perfection by learning to appreciate and to utilize the power of Christ dwelling in your souls as a result of that intimate union of your will with His. You were asked to practice this advertence to His abiding presence even before we establish a more firm conviction of it by a study of the Way of Perfection in the spiritual life.

I now want to emphasize two ideas which may help to increase your enthusiasm for this pursuit. The reason I hope that they will increase your enthusiasm for this pursuit is that they should help to remove the notion that the end which you are seeking, which is no less than sainthood, is aiming so high that is just too discouraging to think of taking it home with you. Perhaps you have already found difficulty in trying to put it into every-day use. In the humdrum of life in the world and in the family, you may have found that your associates and relatives were not yet prepared to accommodate themselves to your sprouting wings. And so you may need a little more help to get started.

The first idea is that I want each of you to begin immediately to say and mean my words of the previous chapter when I said: "In my own life all anxiety for the future or perplexity in the present have practically vanished from my thoughts. They are replaced by a confidence that knows for certain that every detail that unfolds, day by day, and hour by hour, is a part of the mosaic of my life that is composed by God with divine perfection. The result is a peace of soul and an enthusiasm for work which would be impossible in any purely human circumstances of life however consoling they might be."

And I beg you immediately, that you allow to perish the thought that these words are passed down to you from the pinacle of perfection by one who considers himself to have arrived there. Quite the contrary! My enthusiasm stems from the fact that any one as ordinary as I am can find such peace of soul in the practice of the method, regardless of the amount of success.

I have consciously tried to practice what I am preaching to you during the past thirty years. It would be discouraging to you and very false modesty on my part if I should pretend to think that I have had no success in trying to unite my will with that of Christ. But what I want to insist upon is that I am not now, nor have I ever been any different clay from any one of you. My present status is rather that I am at least thirty years along on the road which leads to the conviction that no amount of effort is too much in the pursuit of perfection; no amount of failure is enough to divert one from the pursuit.

This conviction also embraces the assurance that any one can be a full-fledged seeker after sainthood even though one never, in this life, has the consolation of directly conscious supernatural experience. Love and constancy without consolation and in the face of obscurity and dryness are far more pleasing to God than the working of miracles and the heights of ecstacy. Dogged perseverance in seeking and wanting conformity to the will of God, in spite of very little evidence of success, and no mystical experience of union with Christ; these alone are rewarded with that peace of soul of which I speak. Even if no other achievement of perfection is ever sensed in this life, this is worth more than all it can possibly cost! That is what I want to convince you of, and that at least, I can guarantee to each of you from experience.

Furthermore, I want to assure you that life in a monastery is no different, in that regard, from life in any other milieu which brings us shoulder to shoulder with other souls. No matter how holy our associates may be, or however supernatural their motives may be, their actions will have impact upon us which will require the exercise of heroic humility and charity to keep our motive always on a supernatural plane, that is, detached from human emotions of resentment and human inclination to avoid contrariety — to make our responses to be centered on Christ and conformed to His will.

This requires training of our wills because it does not come to us naturally, but only supernaturally. But with the help of Christ, and in spite of lapses, we can train the will just as we train a child to accept disappointment or a hunting dog to concentrate on the game in spite of every distracting commotion.

I only wish that someone had given me the same invitation that I am giving you, about twelve years sooner, so that I could have worked at it with more definite aim during the Catholic part of my married life.

Saint Paul constantly admonished his hearers to be imitators of him as he was an imitator of Christ. He insisted that he was not boasting, but was merely advocating just what I am advocating for you, namely; that you share with me the fun — using Saint Paul's expression — of "putting on Christ." And I humbly repeat with Saint Paul that I am bragging about the universal adaptability of the method, and not the degree of success which I personally have achieved. "Not that I am already perfected; but I press on in the hope of overtaking Him, seeing that I also was overtaken by Christ Jesus. . . . Forgetting what is behind me and reaching out to what is ahead, I press on toward the goal for the prize of the high vocation of God in Christ Jesus. (Eph. 3:12-14).

And this leads up to the second idea which I want to emphasize which is this: each one of you can enroll one hundred percent in the pursuit of perfection and sainthood, here and now, without any anxiety or fear that your friends or relatives will not recognize you when they see you. What I mean is this: The pursuit of sainthood should not be, and is not something so extraordinary that only the most gifted and naturally perfect have any business to think about it. And above all, do not think that it makes one stuffy and uncongenial with one's old associates. The only perceptible change in one who suddenly starts to aim at sainthood is that others gradually begin to wonder how it comes about that they are becoming so much more lovable!

There is a frequently repeated expression: It is all right to honor the saints, but heaven preserve us from having to live with one. That is just plain nonsense! Any one who has a saint for a wife or a sister or mother or father or superior, is lucky, and the saintlier the luckier!

What I have said thus far all boils down to this: The pursuit of sainthood IS for ordinary people. Not only is it for ordinary people, but Christ has definitely made it known that it is a duty of charity for every soul to seek that union with Him which is the very basis of perfection. Christ even goes farther than any purely human director would dare to go. He was talking to the whole body of Christian lay people when He said: "Be ye therefore perfect as also your heavenly Father is perfect." (Matt. 5:48).

The pursuit of sanctity offers the world's best formula for "how to win friends and influence people." It is more highly paid than any other form of human endeavor. And, speaking of influencing people: The apostleship of good example is one of the greatest needs of the Catholic Church in America today. This apostleship begins in the heart of one's home wherever that may be and works out into the whole world. It is the answer to the appeal of our late Holy Father, Pope John XXIII for the prayers of the faithful for Apostolic Spirit in the family. The more we share our Faith with others, the more we increase our own.

The best way to share our faith is to show others what it has done for us, by the example of our goodness. Our intention to do so is the strongest help to make us remember to give that good example at the times when it counts. It is said that every five Jehovah's Witnesses make a convert every year, but it takes two-hundred-and-fifty Catholics to make one convert a year. When one compares what they have to offer with what we have to offer it makes this difference a thousandfold more shocking.

So, having spent a chapter-and-a-half in advertizing our scheme, let us get down to ways and means of putting it into effect. But one last word, to end as we began — the pursuit of sainthood is impossible on our own! It becomes not only possible, but a fascinating vocation in union with Christ.

Now, union with Christ is subject to a vast range of degrees of perfection. In fact, it is this range which may be called the arena wherein our contest will take place. It begins with the purgation of a soul from original sin or mortal sin in the Sacraments of Baptism or Penance and ends with the absolute perfection of the Beatific Vision in heaven. There is no such thing as absolute perfection for us in this world, but this wide space in between is the training school which Saint Paul has likened to the arena wherein, as athletes, we strive after intimate union with Christ. Our final success will fit us for the complete union which is Beatific Vision and the goal of this saint-making theology we are beginning to study.

Practically all my references to God in these pages have been and will be in the name of Christ, the Incarnate Member of the Holy Trinity. In Dogmatic Theology we study the attributes and relationships of the Trinity because all divine acts with respect to creatures stem from the Divine Nature which is shared equally by the Father, Son and Holy Spirit.

But in the saint-making theology which interests us at the moment, it is the Incarnate Member who has taught us all we need to know about the Way of Perfection and who brings with Himself, His Father and His Spirit to abide in our souls and furnish us with the necessary grace to produce

in our souls the end which Saint Paul tersely describes thus:
"For this is the will of God — your sanctification." (I. Thes.
4:3). So, as our study dwells on the central dogma of the Incarnation as the logical source of Christian perfection, we
will never lose sight of the Trinity of Persons in the Unity of
Divine Nature.

There is a delightful and oft-repeated simile which compares our theology of perfection to a beautiful palace standing at the top of a lofty mountain ablaze with a beautiful
mantle of trees and flowers and fruits. The mountain upon
which this palace stands is the revealed word of God, the
Deposit of Faith, the object of Dogmatic Theology which
God has guaranteed for our belief. The fruit which springs
from this foundation of knowledge is the love of God and
respect for neighbor wherein Moral Theology teaches us all
that we *must* do as a product of our knowledge.

The palace is the crowning jewel which invites us to what
we *may* do as a result of our *appreciation* of the fullness of
our knowledge and offers us a thousandfold reward for going
beyond the minimum necessary to preserve our souls in the
atmosphere of divine life.

As we stand at a distance and gaze at this beautiful sight
we are exercising the speculative aspect of this theology of
perfection — we see the dependability of its foundation, the
utility and necessity of its fruit and the immense desirability
of its culmination. In fact, when we realize that all this has
been prepared for us by God, we sense our *obligation* to
strive with all our heart to choose from among the teachings of Christ and of the Church and of the Saints all that
has reference to the perfection of Christian life, and so gain
access to the summit where there is to be found the acme of
delight.

We see also, that the achievement of the summit requires
the careful observance of the rules for the cultivation of the
beauty of the garden on the slopes. In other words, our interest in Moral Theology is not to find out how much we
may steal before we are guilty of mortal sin, or how much
guilt there is in ignorance resulting from sloth. But rather we
will use it as a necessary guide which will enable us to avoid

all sin and start the ascent of this beautiful mountain in complete union with the will of Christ, even as we set foot at the very bottom of its slopes.

Briefly, we will not allow ourselves to be deceived by the notion that we can seek perfection through the practice of the counsels of perfection or seek to practice the highest virtues before we have learned to resist temptation and have at least set about learning how to find the means to avoid all sin.

The mastery of this use of Moral Theology as a guide to aid us over the hard parts of the mountain climb, is what is meant by calling the first stage of our ascent "the purgative way", or the way of beginners. As we learn to use the power of Christ's will to achieve some success in the climb, then we begin to make use of the foundation of Dogmatic Theology. This gives us light to appreciate how our attachment to the Holy Trinity, through Christ and His abiding presence in our souls, gives us power to ascend higher and higher.

Saint Benedict, in the Prologue of his Holy Rule, delights in putting it this way: "As we go forward in our life and in faith, we shall, with hearts enlarged and with unspeakable sweetness of love, run in the way of God's commandments." This stage of our journey in quest of perfection is called "the illuminative way" and gives us the status of "adepts".

Then, as we approach the summit, all influences combine to intensify our love of the indwelling Christ — a love which casts out fear. This love which casts out fear is the source of that incomparable felicity of sensible union with Christ which takes possession of us as we gaze upon the infinite beauty of the many mansions to be seen at the summit. We are then at the threshold of that state which may be enjoyed even in this life through the mystical union with Christ.

This union gives us ever more direct access to His power in ordering every thought and word and act of our lives. This enjoyment of the heights of perfection is called "the unitive way" and those who achieve it are the happy possessors of the most precious felicity to be experienced in this world. They have finished the mountain climb which we are beginning together.

It is a long and arduous climb. Its beginning, as the name implies, involves the necessity of being purged or purified from the purely human and natural motives of our actions. Even the beginning, however, need not be without sweetness, because precisely the same Christ is urging us from within our hearts who will be there all along the way.

Purgation consists of the gradual removal of all that obscurity which dims the constancy of our repose in His embrace. And so it is to increase our enthusiasm for clearing away this dross that we have introduced our subject by taking this quick little look at the final goal.

Another point that should increase our enthusiasm to work hard at the beginning is the consoling thought that these three stages of perfection are not irretrievably isolated from each other. Our quest is a little bit like learning a foreign language, the language of supernatural conversation with Christ. It takes life-long practice to be able to speak without an accent, but even at the very first lesson, we may learn to say "Good morning." Then, with a little more practice, we might learn to say: "I love you." And as we practice it more and more we will learn to mean it as we say it. And when we do this we are really taking little steps in the unitive way. We will, however, have to learn quite a lot more before we understand readily what He says to us. And we will not have a really perfect interchange with Him until we have learned to *think* in the new supernatural language of love. Remember too, that all the time our Teacher rejoices in each new word we learn, more than any loving mother ever rejoiced over the gradual unfolding of that human bond that spoken language gives our hearts.

And so, "Forgetting what is behind me and reaching out to what is ahead, I press on toward the goal for the prize of the high vocation of God which is in Christ Jesus. ("Eph. 3:14).

CHAPTER III

KINDNESS KILLS SADNESS

Did it ever occur to you to speculate as to what this world would be like if all unkindness were removed? The poet has said: "Man's inhumanity to man makes countless thousands mourn." Would you be prepared to go much farther with me and admit that if all unkindness were removed, all sadness would vanish from the world? Perhaps you immediately think: "What about sickness, Father, and what about hunger, and death? How can kindness take away sadness from suffering? " Well, let us examine the evidence together and see if I am going too far.

During the past decade we have all been urged to pray for the fulfillment of the decrees of the Second Vatican Council and especially for the reunion of Christendom. You may have thought: "What can the prayers of one person do to bring the light of faith to five hundred million separated brethren? What can thirty or forty do? " The answer to that is: They would, of course, do nothing at all were it not for the fact that God in His wisdom chooses to manage the world by taking account of every tiny syllable of prayer that comes from the heart of one of His least children. The prayer that you have offered, especially the prayer that you have united with The League Of Prayer For Unity, has become an everlasting part of the bulwark that God is allowing us to share with Him in building against the works of Satan in the world. If you can fully realize this great truth, you will never be anything less than fervent and persevering in prayer. You will never forget that each act of prayer for the welfare of others, when inspired by the love of God, is perhaps worth more for souls than any merely human act of philanthropy can possibly be.

Now, your first thought may be: "Father, aren't you just denying your present thesis when you say that the smallest supernatural act of prayer is worth more than any human act of philanthropy? If prayer is worth more than any human act of kindness, why shouldn't we spend all our time at prayer for others and let God do the rest?" And that is precisely why I have mentioned it in that particular way — to remind you of the contrast between supernatural prayer and natural acts of kindness. My purpose in this chapter is to point out the vast difference between merely human philanthropy and true supernatural kindness which, even more than prayer, or rather as the highest kind of prayer, is truly capable of removing all the sadness from the world.

The famous director of souls, Father Frederick William Faber, preached four sermons on kindness, and he reserved this distinciton between what may be called natural kindness and supernatural kindness until the middle of his fourth conference. I wish to reverse his method and make my case for kindness with a clear understanding at the outset, of the motive which makes it precious in the sight of God. I do this, not as a criticism of Father Faber, but because I believe that in the hundred years since Father Faber preached, we have become accustomed to place far too much emphasis on the adequacy of material acts of philanthropy and far too little regard for honest love of God in our neighbor. The result has been that far too many men of good-will are inclined to view their lives with complacent satisfaction in *doing* good, with never a thought of the necessity of *being* good, to make it count with God. And, by the same token, far too many of those who are not in a position to do good to their neighbor in a notable way, are inclined to exempt themselves from all responsibility for kindness to their neighbor.

A very large percentage of our so-called best people are quite content to consider the acme of perfection as the ethical observance of the Golden Rule with a somewhat distant approbation of the precepts of the Sermon on the Mount. They are content to laud the obvious natural goodness of these precious words of Christ and make a cult of the notions they express without attaching them to their Author. They are deceived into confidence that deeds of benevolence constitute the sum of goodness.

Do not misunderstand me as belittling the great good done by even the most wordly benefactors and contributors to benevolent foundations and Community Chests. I do want you to understand, however, that the kindness which I want us to learn to practice has a very different motive. The donor of a hundred-million dollar foundation *may* be in grave danger of damnation precisely because he has placed his trust in riches and has never learned that they mean nothing to God who has given them. On the other hand, one who has nothing of material value to give, but only kindness to practice, could be aimed at the world's height of perfection.

What, then, is the kindness that we are seeking? It is the expression of pure love bursting the bonds of our mortal frailty. It is more than just charity. It is God's love overflowing from the soul already filled to the brim. The motive power of Divine Charity not only inspires true supernatural kindness, but also colors its every expression and lifts it entirely above the realm of mere philanthropy. The presence of kindness in our treatment of each other offers the possibility of the greatest happiness — its absence invites the greatest unhappiness to souls in this Vale of Tears.

Let us first, then, consider its nature and its expression in thought and word and act, always remembering that we are studying it because it sanctifies the giver and the receiver. We are, therefore, less concerned with its material form than we are with its spiritual results. That is why it is so precious as the key to family happiness.

With that in mind, let us go back to my first question with a better understanding of what I meant by it: Did it ever occur to you to speculate as to what this world would be like if all unkindness were removed? Would you be prepared to admit that all sadness would vanish from the world?

What a weak creature man is when compared with the forces of nature! By himself, how helpless he is against the fury of a hurricane, against the terror of an earthquake, against the awesome suddenness of lightning, against the horrid menace of atomic explosion which now threatens man wherever he may be. Yet, puny as man is before the forces of nature, he has received from God power enough to be the proprietor of this planet. And this power includes as its most precious note the power to make the men of the world happy, or, at the very least, much more happy than they are in this day. This note contained within the power of the men of the world is the power of kindness. It is our treatment of each other that offers the possibility of the greatest happiness and at the same time, is the source of the worst unhappiness and its greatest amount.

The kindness of love drives the Golden Rule into reverse. It urges us to do good to others, not counting on like treatment from them, but overflowing self upon others, informed of their wants by our own yearning for acts of love even though they cannot be returned to us. Christ's parable of the Good Samaritan illustrates *His* meaning of the Golden Rule. He was picturing Himself as the Samaritan doing kindness which could not possibly be repaid by those who received it, but, because of its generosity, bringing joy even though the wounds of the sufferer still remained. In us, the overflow of kindness upon others kills self-love. Self-love is replaced by unselfishness.

In God the first great overflow of self for others began with the creation of the world. It continues with the creation of each individual soul as if the world were all for this new person. His second great overflow of self for others was the giving of Himself to redeem the wreck man had made of the first. And here it should be remembered that beside the sadness that stems from man's unkindness to man, all the sadness of famine, pestilence and other natural evils, stems from man's unkindness to God by sin!

When viewed in this light we can see that God's two great kindnesses furnish an infinite fountain from which flow all the possibilities, all the powers, all the blessings of created kindness. Kindness is our imitation of God's Providence; the outpouring of God's love reflected in His creatures and, as such, the means of quenching all sadness in the world even though part of the suffering must continue until the end of time. If kindness, then, has such tremendous power, we can see that even the little that one soul can do is as important in God's eyes as all the ethically inspired philanthropy in the world. While it may not relieve as much suffering, it has a greater power of removing sadness and of restoring true peace in the world.

Not only does kindness remove sadness from souls — it offsets sin. It tends to deny the frustration of sin and aims the giver and the receiver back toward God's original gift of innocence which is nothing less than the Way of Perfection itself. To quote Father Faber again: "Kindness has converted more sinners than zeal, eloquence or learning, and these can convert no one without kindness. ... The spirit of kindness gains admittance to the souls of men before the doors of which grace has lost its patience and gone away."

Kindness is infectious. It makes the beneficiaries kind. I know of no better illustration than that of the experience of two of the kindest people of my acquaintance. They were on a visiting spree last summer and were spending some of their kindness on the driver of a taxi who was piloting them through Memphis Tennessee on the last day of the annual King Cotton celebration. When the parade prevented him from getting them back to their hotel, he took them on a half-hour sight-seeing tour for which he would take no fee, and he ended by taking them to a lunch-room for coffee, announcing that he wished to be the host since they had not asked for the extra ride nor had they complained of the delay. He said that he needed a rest anyway from the kind of people who were his ordinary fares during King Cotton Week. His last farewell to them was: "Say one for me at

Saint Louis Cathedral in New Orleans." — It was not just *what* happened, but the *way* it happened, and the motive power of supernatural kindness that makes this event important!

How, then, do we learn to make this sort of kindness the mainspring of our family life? First, we must learn to appreciate the stature of kindness among the tools of perfection. Perhaps the best way to approach it is to observe that the habit of kindness in a soul places that soul in an atmosphere where all the virtues are supernaturalized and sanctified. Its expression is towards others but its function is quite as efficacious in behalf of the one possessing it.

It benefits the possessor first because it exterminates selfishness. Furthermore, it tends to propagate itself because of the pleasure it gives, the blessing it draws, and especially because of its likeness to the action of God. The soul possessing the habit of kindness has a special sharing of the Spirit of Jesus. The possession of it alters our viewpoint and makes us hate our selfishness. It carries within itself more than enough grace to make a saint. It is by all odds the most direct road to humility because it is impossible without humility and the pleasure it affords makes humility delightful.

The habit of kindness, however, does not present itself ready-made to beginners in the Way of Perfection. Just as kindness is not a natural trait of youth, so in the spiritual world, kindness is indicative of a degree of maturity of grace. It does not follow, however, that beginners and those not far advanced in perfection are presumptuous to seek to acquire the habit of kindness. In fact, progress in the Way of Perfection is practically impossible without progress in the habit of kindness.

As we have said, the direct effect of kindness is external to the soul who practices it, although its fruits are often quite equally divided between the receiver and the giver. This being true, it should follow that the cultivation of the habit of kindness is most successful and profitable in the area that benefits the giver even more than the receiver; and that is the area of kind thoughts.

Statistics on the matter of Sacramental Confession do not, of course, exist. I believe, however, that there will be little opposition to my surmise that uncharitable thoughts furnish by far the greatest number of items which burden our conscience. This, in itself, should suggest to us that the *substitution* of kind thoughts for unkind ones is the most fertile area in which to begin the cultivation of the habit of kindness. I beg you, however, not to be discouraged by the notion that the effort is hopeless because unkind thoughts are so slippery that they are out before one has time to call a halt. That may be true at first, but remember, I am suggesting the *substitution* of kind throughts for unkind ones as a starter.

One reason why the field of thought is the best place to begin is that it is almost, if not quite, free from the danger of being injured by motives which are less than supernatural. Kind words and kind actions may have their motive marred by human respect, but kind thoughts, since they are known only to God, cannot be thus injured or adulterated. Furthermore, the abundance of occasions for practice makes the field of kind thoughts a sure source of profit. The fact, however, that these occasions for the substitution of kind thoughts for unkind ones, are numerous and are free from danger as to purity of motive, does not mean that the practice is easy, especially at the beginning. In fact, the subtle presence of baser motives may quite often make the practice of kind words and kind actions expedient, but far less profitable spiritually.

Another important point that we must learn when we set out to gain the habit of substituion of kind thoughts for unkind ones, is that it does not admit of exceptions! *Every* time you find yourself having given attention to an unkind thought — and before it finds expression in word or action, deliberately take yourself in hand and substitute a kind thought. Does that sound easy? By no means — but oh so profitable.

And this is especially true when unkind thoughts seem to be thoroughly justified! The substitution of kind thoughts for unkind ones is the surest means of securing complete control of one's thoughts. To quote Father Faber again: "He whose energy covers his thoughts covers the whole extent of self. He has himself completely under his own control, if he has learned to control his thoughts." Father Faber then continues: "The shape of our work and the character of our holiness are regulated from the point at which nature and grace are united. ... But the union of nature and grace is for the most part effected in the world of thought." (Sp. Con. p. 37).

So, it is within our own souls that we must begin to cultivate this precious habit of kindness, where nothing can interfere but our own self-will. But, be warned! Self-will is a formidable adversary at first. Unless one is a solitary hermit, shut sway from all human contracts, one is constantly subjected to temptations to form unkind thoughts and unkind interpretations of the words and acts of others. And, strangely enough, the closest ties of love do not exempt us from these temptations. In fact, the closest family ties produce the most frequent temptations because of the intimate familiarity with the smallest differences of temperament. When these differences appear, the first thoughts can so easily be critical, caustic, sarcastic, clever, ironical, — all of which are unkind.

Moreover, to simply suppress these thoughts without putting them into words or actions, is definitely *not* the proper remedy. No, the only effective remedy is to immediately substitute kind thoughts and kind interpretations; then make them irrevocable by committing them to words and acts. And the more justifiable the unkind thoughts may have been, the more necessary it is to substitute kind thoughts for them and to clinch them with kind words! And by that I do not mean words that are "nasty nice", but words that reflect honest kind thoughts. Difficult? Of course it is difficult, but the cultivation of the spirit of kindness is worth more than all the self-satisfaction of being right and proving it. And this is true even with those whom we are morally bound to guide and correct. As Father Faber puts it: "Hell threatened very kindly is more persuasive than a biting truth about a man's false position." (p. 62).

I have quoted elsewhere an example from my own married life that is so trivial and so much to the point that I am urged to repeat it here: When I was a husband, long before the days of ball-point pens, my precious wife was, perhaps, a little careless about leaving the cap off of her fountain-pen and so she quite frequently had to borrow mine because hers was out of order. Can't you just see the glint in my eye and imagine the ironical phrases that suggested themselves to my mind? What a marvelous opportunity to remember that she did not do it with malice or spite. No, even saints are human.

And so it is with me today. Every family of Religious as well as every family in the world, is bristling with opportunities to substitute kind thoughts and kind interpretations for critical ones. This is emphasized for Monks because so may of our words and acts are done as part of the corporate action of our liturgical functions. But here again, everyone can be assumed to be aiming at sainthood so mistakes and mannerisms are not grounded in malice, but rather are items of personality and so are very much adapted to kind interpretations. So you see, the closer we are to others, in family or profession, the greater the opportunity to profit by these occasions that invite the practice of the supernatural charity of kindness.

Kind words long practiced are the only sure remedy for deep-seated misunderstandings. They not only avoid and heal evil, but they positively produce happiness. We who are steadfastly faithful are sometimes amazed at the blindness of those who fall away; let us not be equally blind in ourselves to the precious graces of kindness. After all, it *is* easily practiced if we set about it with steadfast determination to cooperate with grace... "There seems to be an almost universal fallacy among mankind," says Father Faber, "which leads them to put a higher price on kindness than it deserves."

Hence, the effect of kindness received is out of all proportion to the amount of kindness done! It spreads from one to many and becomes self-propagating. It promotes sanctity, and sanctity kills sadness. Let us, then, take advantage of this fallacy and do our part to kill the sadness in the world, in accordance with the admonition of Saint Paul to the Ephesians: "There must be no trace of bitterness among you, of passion, resentment, quarelling, insulting talk, or spite of any kind; be kind and tender to one another, each of you generous to all, as God in Christ has been generous to you (4:31-32).

CHAPTER IV

LIVING FAITH AND PERFECTION

As we seek to answer the invitation to practice the virtue of supernatural kindness, we must advert to the utter necessity of help from God and remember that confidence on our part is the key to that help. Nowhere is this thought better expressed than in the words of the thirty-second psalm: "Patiently we wait for the Lord's help; He is our strength and our shield; in Him our hearts find contentment, in His Holy Name we trust. Lord, let Thy mercy rest upon us, who put all our confidence in Thee. (20-22).

And so, let us examine the source of that confidence. We are accustomed to speak of the three theological virtues — Faith, Hope and Charity. It is my hope that in this chapter we may discover that for us, who are seeking to pursue the Way of Perfection, these virtues are not as different as their names might tend to make them seem, but rather, they are three interlocking parts of that priceless Christian possession, supernatural confidence in God. Now, while confidence in God may be called the outcome or evidence of the possession of the theological virtues, it also involves of necessity many other things almost equally important.

First and foremost, it involves utter contentment and enjoyment of the indwelling presence of God in one's soul, without which it cannot even begin to exist. Then, with that as equipment, one is admitted into full membership includ-

ing an unlimited drawing account on the treasures of God's
Providence. This also includes the solution of every encoun-
ter with the "Problem of Evil" and, less dramatic but perhaps more important than all else, it supplies the order of
everything we do. It is easy to see that this subject would
supply material for several volumes instead of one chapter of
this book. So, I will limit my treatment of the subject of
confidence in God to the single aspect of its precious day-
by-day and hour-by-hour and minute-by-minute application
to every thought and word and act of each one of us.

In the previous chapter I asked you to relish with me the
precious habit of supernatural kindness. I have said that my
enthusiasm stems from the fact that it offers such frequent
opportunities in the Way of Perfection. Please do not think
that I am fickle when I say that the subject of this chapter
thrills me more than all the rest put together because its application is not just frequent; it fills all the time there is in
one's life! The habit of supernatural kindness, which fills
me with enthusiasm just as much as it ever did, is not really
an accomplishment in its own right, but rather, it is one of
the happier manifestations of supernatural confidence in
God. The habit of kindness is, in fact, quite impossible to
acquire or to use unless it stems from that ever-present confidence in God.

There is a prayer to Mary which appears in prayer books
as a morning prayer, but since it is really an elaboration of
the "Hail, Mary", I like to recite it many times each day:

> "O Mary, my Mother, I commend to thy blessed faithful-
> ness, to thy safe-keeping, and to the haven of thy loving
> kindness, my soul and my body, this day and every day
> and in my last hour. All my hope and consolation; all my
> cares and miseries; all my life, and my life's end, I commit
> to thee and by thy merits and most holy intercession do
> thou direct and order all my doings in accordance with
> the will of thine only Son."

The reason I like this prayer especially is that it ties the
notion of Mary's mediation into the notion of confidence in
God, without which Mary's mediation is meaningless. Thus,
it brings Mary and Jesus, by faith, into every act of life. In
other words, it reminds me that confidence in God is noth-

ing else but *living faith*. And, whereas I have called supernatural kindness the "key to perfection", I should say that
this perfect confidence in God *is* the Way of Perfection itself. This should help us to understand how important it is.

No one who has true confidence in God, which is truly
living faith, could possibly fall away. One might almost say
that truly living faith is incompatible with moral sin. The
reason is that truly living faith is an uninterrupted contact
with the indwelling presence of God in the soul. To deliberately drive God out by mortal sin could only mean that
true confidence in His presence had never made that contact
real and vibrant with life, but only an artificial and tentative
thing. The grace of faith is a gift from God, but the intensity of its living quality comes from our cooperation with
that grace which gives it form. In heaven sin will be impossible because the curtain of faith will be drawn aside in the
Beatific Vision, but here, it is our life work to make that veil
thin by using the help of God to make that faith live.

Furthermore, the negative power of living faith which
protects us against temptation and helps us to keep away
from sin, is only half of its treasure. It is the positive quality
of living faith which gives us the greatest incentive to work
at it. It is what I have called an unlimited drawing account
on the treasures of God's Providence which supplies us with
the solution of every problem of life, directs the order of
everything we do, and, best of all, brings happiness into all
of it — even our brushes with the problem of evil.

Every priest and Religious is constantly reminded of the
truth of this idea because of our daily recitation of the
Divine Office which is saturated with it from the Book of
Psalms which is one long rhapsody of praise and thanksgiving
for the utter completeness of God's Providence. The text
which I have quoted from the thirty-second psalm is only a
tiny sample of the fullness of God's invitation for us to turn
to Him in every need. I might just as well have quoted Psalm
Ninety, which we used to recite every day in choir the last
thing before retiring: "He trusts in Me, mine it is to rescue
him; he acknowledges My Name, from Me he shall have protection; when he calls upon Me, I will listen, in affliction I

am at his side, to bring him safety and honor. Length of days he shall have to content him, and find in Me deliverance." (14-16).

There are dozens of other selections which are equally inviting, but I want to quote just one more because it introduces that counterpart of confidence which is fear of the Lord. This quotation is taken from Psalm One-Hundred-Twenty-Seven which we used to recite every week-day morning: "Blessed art thou, whoever thou art that fearest the Lord, that walkest in His ways ... blessed shalt thou be and it shall be well with thee." (Ps. 127:1-2). The fear here mentioned is not servile fear, but it is the fear which is referred to in Psalm One-Hundred-Ten as "the beginning of wisdom." (Ps. 110:10). And in Ecclesiasticus as the beginning of love: "The fear of God is a gift beyond all gifts; blessed the man that receives it, he has no equal. Fear the Lord and thou shalt learn to love Him; cling close and thou shalt learn to trust Him." (25:14-16).

This fear is very different from fright. It is really the fruit of true appreciation of the majesty of God and wondering love and gratitude for His condescension in coming to dwell in one's soul when one is in a state of grace. It is the attitude of a soul fully equipped to enjoy God's Providence. And, by enjoying God's Providence, I mean finding joy in every single thing that happens because it is known to be within the protecting wing of His almighty power.

With all this in mind, then, let us examine our concept of God's Providence with a view of entering into this enjoyment of it. First, by way of emphasis, let us imagine ourselves in a situation that will enable us, at it were, to rate ourselves in the exercise of confidence in God.

In the eighth chapter of the Gospel of Saint Matthew, there is described a test of confidence which God provided for the disciples who were sailing across the Sea of Galilee with the Savior. He was asleep on a cushion in the after part of the ship when a storm became so violent that the ship was being swamped by the waves. Seeing that the ship was on the point of sinking, the disciples, in their last extremity, turned to Him in whose power to save them they had implicit confidence, and cried to Him for help. Under ordinary circumstances the crew of a ship which was foundering in a storm, would pay scant attention to a nonseafaring passenger asleep in the stern. No, the only reason they turned to Him was that they had perfect confidence in His ability to cope with the situation which to them seemed otherwise hopeless. He immediately rose and justified their confidence by quenching the storm and so saved their lives.

But what did He say to them first? "Why are you afraid, you men of little faith? " One almost has to suppress a little chuckle in wondering what would have been the sequel if they *had* shown such strong faith as to allow Him to sleep on undisturbed. There is, however, a perfectly marvelous lesson for us in this incident. And, like everything else in God's management of this world, it is easy to see that our loving Savior was addressing us in this little reproach, more directly than He was chiding those who had really given a keen proof of their perfect faith in Him.

The life of each one of us today has many qualities which can be compared with a voyage at sea in a sailing vessel. Sometimes the going is smooth and easy, sometimes the winds are contrary and much care is required to make headway, sometimes the sun and stars are obscured and it is hard to know what course to steer, sometimes a storm comes up and the situation seems utterly hopeless. Christ is always present, as it were, asleep on the cushion in the after part of the boat, just at our finger tips.

He is even closer to us than He was to the disciples in their boat on the Sea of Galilee. He is right inside of us, sharing our soul and supernaturalizing it. There is no temptation, there is no hardship, there is no evil done to us, there is no accident or sickness or calamity which may befall us, there is no bereavement which we may suffer, but He is aware of every tiny detail of it and able and willing to prevent it if need be for our good. He is just as truly present to us as He was to His disciples on the boat in the storm. The only difference is that now we cannot touch Him with our hands or see Him rise and master the situation; we must exercise a degree of faith which He regretted that He did not find in His terrified disciples.

We must have that confidence in Him which fights its way through every obscurity and stands firm in living faith. When we have learned to do this we have solved every problem which has ever been met by any saint, along the Way of Perfection. This sounds quite simple but it is not. The reason it sounds so simple is that I have made it seem like an entirely passive operation which it is not. It is true that absolutely everything that happens to us is under the complete control of Christ. It is also true that He has complete control of the result of everything that we do in response to what happens to us. But He refuses to allow our response to be a purely passive matter. We are not permitted to be like the rest of creation, compelled to act according to the law of our nature.

Quite the contrary, we may be said to be compelled by God to make a positive choice in everything about our life that makes God love us. He controls every minute detail of the results of our choices, but He refuses always to interfere with the freedom of our will. He will even stand aside and allow us the utter folly of making our souls inhospitable to His presence by mortal sin.

So, we can easily see that there is just one barrier to the mass-production of saints according to the benign operation of Divine Providence. That barrier is the perverse opposition of the human will to the will of God, and it stems from the blunting of that living faith which makes God the ever-present Protector of our souls. How, then, since it is so all-important, are we to avoid this blunting of our faith and instead, build up such confidence in God that it will make us saints? First of all, we must know that this very confidence itself is a precious item of God's Providence. It is, therefore, a supernatural grace that is a gift from God, but more than any other grace, it has the nature of an acquisition, something we can work at, and must work at, if we are to make any progress in perfection.

This world we live in is, let's face it, a "vale of tears", made so by the perversity of man. Every human being born of woman is surrounded by sin, sorrow, and suffering. Especially is this true in our day when every nation in the world is being eaten away by the cancer of Atheistic Materialism which withers love. How can I reconcile this with the utter confidence of living faith which I have said is due to almighty God who has complete control of every tiny thing that happens? Our Catechism tells us that God created the world a garden of delight. It was man, who, by the abuse of the free-will given to him by God, has changed it into a vale of tears, made so, not only by man's inhumanity to man, but also by man's ingratitude to God which has earned sickness, suffering and death. Or, as Saint Paul puts it: "The Scripture hath imprisoned all things under sin." (Gal. 3:22). And, in his Epistle to the Romans, he says: "Created nature has been condemned to frustration, not for some deliberate fault of its own, but for the sake of him who so condemned it with a hope to look forward to; namely, that nature in its turn will be set free from the tyranny of corruption." (Rom. 8:20-21). All that is evil, both physical and moral, stems from man's rebellion all along the line.

Must we say, then, that God's wonderful plan was botched by man? That is certainly what many of our Catechism answers seem to imply. And that is what any one of us with living faith should steadfastly deny! Do I mean to say, then, that God *likes* the world as it is? — that God likes the sin that has caused all the evil? No! God hates sin and could easily have prevented every vestige of it. But, in His wisdom, He allows it only because He is so jealous of our free-will that He will let the whole world fall apart, if need be, to keep what makes us lovable to Him, that living faith that trusts Him, *come what may*! We must believe that all things do work together for good to those who put their trust in God. He has given us ample assurance that His promises cannot fail, but He insists that "what was promised must be given through faith in Jesus Christ."

After all, we must admit that it is by trials that God shows us our own weakness and proves His power to bring good out of every evil that He allows to occur. My own life would have been a very different affair if God had let me be the chooser of the events that had most to do with shaping it as I mentioned in Chapter One — a Catholic for the wife of a militant Protestant and a widower at age fifty-three.

God has chosen the trials which He has planned for each one of you. They are different from mine, but they are just as real. They express God's will for you. He asks you to meet them all with the trust of living faith. As the Holy Spirit has inspired the author of the Book of Proverbs to say: "Put all your heart's confidence in the Lord, on thy own skill rely never; wilt thou but keep Him in thy thoughts wherever thou goest, He will show thee the straight path." (Prov. 3:5).

And so it is with *all* that seems evil in this world. It *is* as God has planned it to be, a vale of tears, to temper our free-will into love. Saint Augustine has put it perfectly. He says: "Almighty God preferred to bring good out of evil than never to allow evil to occur."

Let us, then, take this as a lesson for every day of our lives: However fierce the storm, however high the waves, we are never facing them alone; Christ is no longer sleeping on the cushion in the stern. No, He is standing by, within our souls ready to help us whenever we turn to Him. All the trials, all the suffering in the world, if accepted with utter living faith and confidence in God, and in union with Christ, make this world what God intended it to be — *a launching-pad for heaven!*

CHAPTER V

GRACE FOR EVERY DAY

If any of you ever attend a marriage at which I am the assisting priest, you will hear me address the bride and groom with words hopefully planned to burn into their souls a lively appreciation of the wedding gift which each of them, by the power of God, has bestowed upon the other. I will do my best to make them know beyond the shadow of a doubt that however many or however precious any other gifts may be, not one of them, nor all of them combined, can compare with the value to each of them of the blessed treasure of the grace of the Sacrament of Marriage.

Lovely household goods and table-ware can certainly add delight to the festive beginnings of married life. A good bank account and a well paid position give a sense of security that may add joy to the prospects for the future. But these may be lacking, or, having been obtained, may be lost, without being allowed to mar the joy of the bride and groom having each a key to the treasure-chest of Sacramental Grace.

Now, your first thought probably is: Don't they all have the same Sacramental Grace, and isn't it kind of nice to have the other things too? It is the answer to that question, applied not only to the Sacrament of Marriage, but to all sacramental grace, that I wish to make the subject of this chapter. Yes, those who receive the sacraments, *do* all have the same grace given to them, but the use they make of it varies as much as does the success of their vocation, whatever it may be.

In Chapter Three, I asked you to learn with me to use the healing balm of supernatural kindness. I went so far as to insist that, if all unkindness were banished from the world, all sadness would vanish with it. I emphasized the importance of the efforts of each individual soul in this regard, and I suggested that the best way to make the practice of kindness a habit is to be on guard to replace every unkind thought that enters one's mind with a kind thought and then clinch it with a kind word even though the unkind thought may have been justified.

I suggested also that the best place to cultivate this habit is in the bosom of one's own family, because there the intimacy of life makes the need for kindness more constant and familiarity makes the temptations to neglect kindness more treacherous. I urged you to work very hard to gain this habit of kindness, calling it the key to perfection. I even told you that I thought that the notion of kindness as the key to perfection was the most useful topic we had considered together up to that point.

Then, in Chapter Four, I apparently repudiated all my fine praise of the habit of kindness by telling you that the acme of perfection is to be found only in that living faith which begets a perfect confidence in God. I even insisted that that notion was worth all my previous writings put together, although I did defend my former enthusiasm for the habit of kindness, saying it was just as strong as ever, but that kindness is really just a top-drawer expression of confidence in God.

I now want to confess that both of those chapters were addressed to myself just as much as they were addressed to you. I have a considerable and not altogether successful battle on each count. I realized the essential truth of what I was telling you and telling myself at the same time, but I have been disturbed by the fact that the telling of it and the believing of what I was telling, did not automatically make me able to substitute kind thoughts for unkind ones, nor did it reinforce my confidence in God to the point where I felt

sure that I would be any less terrified than were the disciples
of Christ when their ship began to sink as they were crossing
the Sea of Galilee with the Savior.

So, having made that confession, I want to share with
you the progress which I have made in finding the answer.
The solution, I believe, to success in the art of acting with
supernatural kindness and of making it a true manifestation
of living faith, is to be found in the possessive use of the
graces given us by our Lord Jesus Christ. And most precisely
is it found in the sacramental graces which Christ has provided to make perfection the natural goal of every state of
live.

Priests and Religious are said to have made a profession
of the Way of Perfection. People who live in the world are
often inclined to allow themselves to slip into the notion
that they are automatically detached from the Way of Perfection as soon as they are, of necessity, thrust into the day-
by-day distractions or temptations which accompany house-
keeping, family raising, social events, earning a living, or anything else connected with just being in the world.

When you make a retreat, or even a brief day of recollection, you are, perhaps, helped to get a glimpse of the near-
ness of Christ and to rejoice in the intimate love which He
has for you and for your individual affairs. You perhaps
think, a little wistfully: Oh, if I could only take Him home
with me and keep Him all year long! Perhaps you are inclined to think that priests or Religious are to be envied a
little because it is so easy for them to do just that. But I
want to tell you that, if any of them are better off in that
regard, it is chiefly because they have, perhaps, become a
little more expert than you in using the *means* of keeping
that contact close.

The means of perfection are graces, or helps from God,
without which no one can take one step in the Way of Perfection; no one can even aim at Sainthood. But, I want to
insist right here on three things especially for you: first,
these graces or helps are just as much available to you as
they are to any priest or Religious, or any saint for that
matter; second, they can and must be taken home with you

and used all day long, every day; third, everyone can be a
saint who will use the graces which God always *offers*. The
only reason that there may be more saints among religious
than among lay people is that a religious vocation itself is
one of the fruits of willingness to use grace. It is no easier,
however, to use grace in the cloister or the rectory or the
Abbey than it is in the home. I want you to know that you
can take the retreat atmosphere home with you and keep it
fresh all year long, but only by *using* grace.

Now, you may think: well I have tried to do that after
every chapter of this book but I always lapse back into the
world in a very short time. And so, I want to tell you just
what I mean by "using" grace. First let us recall just what
we mean by the word "grace". Our Catechism uses the name
"grace" for two things which are quite different from each
other. First, there is Sanctifying, or saint-making Grace
which is a quality or state of the soul brought about when
God takes up His abode in the soul, making one a child of
God instead of a child of wrath. As I have explained in
Chapter Seven of *HOW COME MY FAITH?* , this quality or
state of saint-making grace is a supernatural and free gift
from God that comes to us at Baptism and continues
throughout life unless God is driven out of the soul by mortal sin. In that event sanctifying grace is totally lost. It is
God's presence or absence that determines whether a person
is, or is not, in a state of grace.

On the other hand, we speak correctly of obtaining an *increase* of sanctifying grace. In fact, the storing within our
souls of a lifetime harvest of saint-making grace is the main
purpose of our creation and the most important work we do
in this world. It is to be our eternal retirement fund; we
cannot draw on it in this life, but that does not lessen its
value, but rather, increases it because our wealth of saint-
making grace will be the sole measure of our state in heaven.
Saint-making grace is, therefore, quite different from the so-
called helping graces or actual graces given by the sacraments
which are the main topic of this chapter. Saint-making grace
is, perhaps, best described as a capacity to love God, a skill,
one might say, in giving glory to God, and so a measure of

our ability to enjoy the Beatific Vision in heaven. As I have said, we cannot draw upon it in this world because it is like a trust estate which is to be placed at our disposal only at the judgment seat of God.

We can, however, and do determine its size by all our acts in this world which either build it up or tear it down, or forfeit our right to it altogether. This little explanation should help us to have a better understanding of three things: first, why those who have a true understanding of the meaning of saint-making grace have such a destestation of mortal sin in particular, and all sin in general; second, what is meant by the salutation "full of Grace" which was addressed to the Blessed Virgin by the angel Gabriel, and; third, why the hoarding of saint-making grace offers a motive far stronger than merely keeping out of hell.

It is the understanding of this last notion which prompts men and women to leave the world and devote their lives exclusively to God's service. It also prompts those who remain in the world to use all the means provided by God to increase saint-making grace and to accept trials and temptations and disappointments almost with gratitude, since they are the God-chosen sources of special dividends of saint-making grace. But, above all, it prompts everyone to learn to make the fullest use of what might be called the spending-money of supernatural life which is offered to all according to their needs. This spending money is the supernatural help of actual grace which can be used here and now and is the sole medium of exchange which one can use to increase his capital fund of saint-making grace.

Now, certain actual graces are offered even to those who have made themselves God's enemies by mortal sin, inviting them to come back to the fountains of life which Christ has provided for the lambs and sheep of His flock. But, by far the greatest fund of actual graces is to be found in these fountains themselves — the seven sacraments, each of which is the source of a limitless supply of actual grace for every special need of life in the world, and each is also a source of saint-making grace of which God has made it the carrier and cause.

Now, it is said that the sacraments confer grace *"ex opere operato"*. That means that they infuse grace into the soul by the very working of the sacrament itself. Two of them, Baptism and Penance, even bring the living God into a soul which is supernaturally dead; all of them give some increase of saint-making grace whenever they are worthily received. But, as to the actual or sacramental grace of special virtue for each sacrament, I have designedly used the word "offered". It is, of course, true that sacramental grace is also contained in each sacrament *ex opere operato*, but actual grace does not function except with the cooperation of the soul into which it is infused. And that is what accounts for the difference in results experienced by those to whom the sacraments are given. It accounts for the dismal failure of some marriages as compared with the brilliant success of others, even those involving the most difficult problems. Sacramental grace may be thought of as given to one in a purse which must be opened and the grace taken out by the free will before it begins to operate.

It reminds me of the unique experience which I reported in Chapter Seven of *A REBEL FROM RICHES*, when I was building a gasoline plant in Breckenridge, Texas. It was in 1920 when the Breckenridge Field was just emerging as an oilfield after three years of drought which had reduced the few remaining cattle farmers to a state of pitiful poverty.

As our pipeline crew were connecting a very rich discovery well to our gas gathering line, the owner of the farm on which the well was located came out in very dilapidated dress and asked if he could have some of the money which had been promised to him if oil was discovered. In amazement the foreman went with him to his poverty-stricken house and was shown three production statements which the owner had not recognized as royalty checks totalling over fifty thousand dollars!

Too many of us allow the riches of sacramental grace to stand on the shelf unused, while we struggle along at snail's pace on the Way of Perfection making grace a burden instead of a precious asset. Partly through ignorance of its presence; partly through ignorance of the necessity of cashing the checks or opening the purse and taking it out to use; partly through failure to prize eternal values in competition with the momentary satisfactions of pride, concupiscence, envy, impatience, and lack of charity; we miss golden opportunity after golden opportunity to store up treasure in heaven.

In retreats and days of recollection we receive the impulses that set the pace for us on the Way of Perfection, but it is sacramental grace that can keep us going at full speed during all the time that comes in between. It is sacramental grace that can keep us earning merits in the face of leaky faucets, broken windows, trials of patience, failings of our dear ones, not to mention the real calamities that Christ may allow to enter our lives. There are seven sacraments which Christ has provided to furnish us with every kind of grace we need whenever we need it.

I mentioned the grace of the Sacrament of Marriage at the beginning of this chapter because it is, perhaps, the most specialized grace of all and because, except for the grace of the Sacrament of Orders, it has the most tricky and special office to perform. The vocation of marriage is filled with wonderful consolations, but it is also punctuated with an amazing variety of trials and situations demanding charity, kindness, tact, and confidence in God. Sacramental grace is required to meet all these situations successfully. But Sacramental grace does not automatically step in and remedy these situations as they occur. It is there and it is sufficient, but you must think to use it. All it takes is just a little act of the will with a glance toward God, but you will sometimes have to push through a surge of impatience or real anger to get at it. Every time you do use it successfully you will become more skilled in turning to it quickly.

I have asked you to practice the substitution of kind thoughts for unkind ones; then, in the next chapter I asked you to strengthen your ability to do this by anchoring your confidence in God to a *living* faith. Every time you have done either you have used sacramental grace. If you have not succeeded as well as you might wish, it is because you have not yet become skillfull in drawing on your treasure of sacramental grace.

I also asked you in Chapter Ten of *LET'S MEND THE MESS!* to become an apostle of the Sacrament of Penance for yourself and for all those whom you might be able to influence. While the essential purpose of the Sacrament of Penance is to restore life to those who are dead in spirit, for you who are seeking to follow the Way of Perfection, it is a most important source of another kind of sacramental grace. This grace might be called the "Repair kit" for every kind of imperfection and venial sin, but it too, has to be opened and used in order to produce results. The grace of the Sacrament of Penance is the ever-ready instrument for perfecting and straightening the wrinkles in everyday life.

The most precious sacrament of all, and the one which supplies the power of all the rest, is, of course, the Blessed Sacrament of the Body and Blood of Christ. No human being who believes in the reality of this Sacrament can fail to understand its preciousness. There is, however, a real danger that our zest for it can be blunted by the scandal of those who cheat themselves of it by choosing for themselves a state of mortal sin. It seems incredible that anyone could be so indifferent to the riches of this Sacrament of Christ's love. The only answer can be that God allows the first beginnings of self-love to blunt the understanding of those who prefer self-indulgence to God's law. Make no mistake! — there is not one of us who is not vulnerable to injury from this scandal.

And so, I beg you who have faithfully tried to follow the Way of Perfection, to carry your fervor throughout the days ahead by continued access to the bountiful treasury of sacramental grace which is offered you day by day for every need, first and foremost, in the grace of frequent Mass and Communion and frequent recourse to the Sacrament of Penance, remembering too, to use the graces of your special state to make this life happier and heaven more glorious.

> **"By the Grace of God I am what I am, and the grace He infused into me has not been void: I have worked harder than all of them, or rather, it was not I but the Grace of God working with me." (I. Cor. 15:10).**

CHAPTER VI

A NEW ADVENT IN THE LIVES OF MEN

Each of my books has one chapter devoted to some phase of the influence of the Blessed Virgin Mary in our pursuit of the Way of Perfection. Each year there seems to me to be a more urgent reason to emphasize the wish of Christ, the God-Man, that we should take a more living share of the grace that He offers us through His Mother. He has made her our Mother and our Mediatrix to bring us to Him so that He may bring us to perfection and present us to His Father in heaven.

It is true that our souls are prepared for heaven by the indwelling presence of the Triune God and Mary does not dwell within the soul. She does, however, in accordance with God's will, have a major role in bringing about that indwelling Presence within us. It is, therefore, most appropriate that we should think of it in that light in this final book of the series (of five). Just as Christ, the God-Man grew to natural perfection in the body of Mary, so does she, in her role as our supernatural Mother of Grace, secure for us who are her children, such grace that the God-Man grows to supernatural perfection within the soul of each one of us.

It is in this light that I wish to suggest an attitude of mind that will hasten this supernatural building of Christ within us. Then He may come to birth for us on Christmas Day in a manner which is very real, as all supernatural events must be. He will then live within us in close union during the Christmas and Epiphany Seasons; He will cause us to share with Him the sacrifice of suffering and death by which He won our salvation during the Penitential Season; and His Spirit will return and dwell with us to lead us on to perfection at His Resurrection.

It is His wish that all this should come about for us in close union with His Mother as our Mediatrix of grace and, above all, as our example of perfection. This can come about in us as in the Season of Advent which brings to us the great miracle of the Incarnation. And Mary will hasten the growth of Christ within us provided we will let her have full sway within our souls as *a new advent in the lives of men.* She will also see that we will be well rewarded.

Let us, then, begin at this moment to let Christ grow in our bodies and souls in a really sincere and intentional imitation of her response: "Fiat mihi secundum verbum tuum" — "Be it done to me according to Thy word." And let us be assured that it is God's pleasure that it shall actually take place within us to the extent that we advert to her help and imitate her actions.

And, when I speak of imitation of her actions, I am reminded of a delightful paragraph in the introduction to an equally delightful little book about the Blessed Virgin by Caryll Houselander, entitled, *THE REED OF GOD.* The author recalls that, as a child, she was told that all the angels in heaven would blush if she did anything that Our Lady would not do. She goes on to say: "It was clear to me that all those things which spelt joy to me were from henceforth taboo — blacking my face with burnt cork, turning somersaults between the props against the garden wall, putting two bull's-eyes into my mouth at the same time — all that was over! But even if I faced a blank future shackled with respectability, it was still impossible to imagine Our Lady doing anything that I would do, for the very simple reason that I could not imagine Our Lady doing *anything at all.*"

Is it not true that the same childish image is all too apt to be repeated in the mind of any one of us? Our Christmas cards, our icons, our statues, even the stable at Bethlehem or

the flight into Egypt, pictures her in an immaculate, long
flowing garment with every fold in perfect order and no re-
minder of anything but calm adoring repose. Indeed, I suppose this is as it should be since I always shudder when I see
attempts to modernize the pictures of Our Lady.

The Bible texts, however, which relate to the Blessed
Virgin give almost the opposite impression. After the appearance of the Angel Gabriel, who brought her the precious
news that she was to be the Mother of God, we could easily
imagine that she would retire in ecstatic reverie to adore the
thought of God born in her. But, what do we find? Instead,
unmindful of self and the unprecedented dignity which had
been conferred upon her, she thinks only of the plight of
her elderly cousin Elizabeth who, far beyond the normal age
of motherhood, must need sympathy and encouragement as
well as house-keeping help, with child-birth less than three
months away.

The brief words of Saint Luke's Gospel only half do justice to the event: "And Mary rose up and went with all
haste to a town of Juda in the hill country where Zachary
dwelt; and there entering she gave Elizabeth greeting." (Luke
1:39). The text gives the impression that she went alone although it is almost unbelievable that a young girl would start
out alone on an eighty-five mile hike over the same territory
in which the Good Samaritan rescued the man who fell
among thieves. It was no small undertaking in any case. This
was followed by three months of help for her cousin and
then again the same journey back to Nazareth, since it was
then necessary for her to be in Joseph's care lest she be
stoned to death when her pregnancy became evident.

But all that was far less arduous than the same trip made
on the very eve of her own "blessed event" when the roads
and all the stopping places were teeming with caravans of
people going to their tribal headquarters in response to the
command of Emperor Augustus for the census. Neither of
these events, however, compared with the momentous one
when Joseph came to Mary while they were living in
Bethlehem and said that he had been warned in a dream that
they must take the precious Child and leave, not just

"soon", but that night, immediately, for Egypt, over two-hundred miles of almost waterless desert which was notorious as a hide-out of every sort of lawless men. It seemed like madness, but Mary's utter trust in God left no indecision for her in this unexpected turn of events. She quietly obeyed and thus saved the life of the God-Child.

Indeed, all life long, Mary's life was action; sometimes quiet simple action; always with a single purpose; to live, to die if need be, for the Life that had taken His human form from her and continued all her life to live in her. It is because of her perfect fulfillment of this mission given her by God that He chose her to be our Mother also, to bring Christ to birth in us by the power of the Holy Spirit and to cause Him to remain in us all life long to transform our life into His. In other words, Christ brought to us by Mary will enable us to do in every act of life what Mary would do, whether it be the quiet simple acts of every-day living or the heroic and difficult acts that God may choose to ask of us during this difficult time in the history of the world.

We can do this just as Mary did it, by living the life of Jesus within us. Furthermore, God has helped to make this possible for us by giving us first, the example of Mary, and then, by giving her to us to take charge of the doing of it for us and to obtain for us the grace to do it all "gracefully."

The beautiful prayer to Our Lady, attributed to Saint Aloysius Gonzaga, which I quoted in Chapter Four, reminds us of this with such devotion and simplicity and grace that it has for years inspired me to recite it many times every day. This prayer reflects beautifully the role of Mary in our lives which God is teaching us to cherish by the events taking place in our generation. This is the age which contains the apparitions of Lourdes and of Fatima and the declaration of her Immaculate Conception and her Assumption into Heaven. It comes as a slight surprise, therefore, to realize that Saint Aloysius' prayer was popular with the faithful as far back as the sixteenth century. It only shows, however, that those who have known God's will, in every century have always known what He meant when He said to Saint

John, "Behold thy Mother" and that she well knew what He meant when He said to her, "Mother behold thy son."

The sentiment of this prayer of Saint Aloysius came to vibrant life again one hundred years later when, at the beginning of the eighteenth century, Saint Louis Montfort conceived his "True Devotion to Mary," which is so popular today and which inspires her cult in the Legion of Mary and among many other groups of Religious. We can now see in retrospect that God chose Saint Aloysius and Saint Louis de Montfort as heralds of the glories of Mary with which God planned to remind our generation of the importance of her part in the economy of our salvation.

It is most important for us to advert to these reminders in these years since the Second Vatican Council. Anti-Priests and other haters of the Church have succeeded in diminishing devotion to Mary and quenching the Rosary in many areas. This success comes straight from hell and should be abhorred by every loyal *Mender*.

But, aside from these devilish machinations, I want to ask you to notice in particular that, always and everywhere, Mary is represented as our most loving Mediatrix and Intercessor and Mother. It is her function as our Mother, to build Christ in us. Especially in this season of attack from Anti-Priests we should think of Christ coming to birth in us through the good offices of our Mother — "by thy most holy intercession do thou direct and order all my doings in accordance with the will of thine only Son."

It is by the power of the Holy Spirit that she is given the office of building the presence of her Son in us, just as through the same Holy Spirit she nourished His natural body into life. If we learn to think of her in that capacity, we will also learn to think and speak and act as she did because we will be acutely aware that we are mothers of Christ in the sense that Christ meant when He said: "Whoever does the will of My Father who is in heaven, he is my Mother." (Matt. 12:50).

When a mother is nourishing the body of a child within her she has very few thoughts or acts which are wholly detached from that new life for which she is giving herself.

With Mary, added to that natural mother-love and devotion, was that precious knowledge that *this* new life within her was that of the most high God. Naturally she was constantly and intensely aware of *His* presence, and equally naturally, this made it impossible for her to divert her will away from His will. So, if we will let her do for us what God has told us that He wishes her to do, we will have no less incentive than she did to be mindful of that new life growing within us.

She will start Him there as if by a seed, as He Himself loved to explain in His parables about the kingdom of heaven. Or, as I like still better to think, she will let us sense His presence in us as the bud of a fragrant rose which will only yield its sweetest perfume as we take it with us into heaven. There is no comparison, however, which can have a more fruitful impact upon our actions, day-by-day and minute-by-minute, than the perfectly legitimate thought of the God-Man coming to birth within us.

I call this a perfectly legitimate thought because of the words of Saint Paul addressed to the Galatians: "My little children, with whom I am again in travail until Christ be formed in you." (Gal. 4:19). These words have much more than a symbolic meaning. The Spirit of Christ does actually come to be formed in the body of each one of us, as in a tabernacle, by the supernatural intervention of the Holy Spirit and the loving intercession of the Blessed Virgin. The important difference, however, is that, being wholly supernatural, the fruition of this operation in our lives depends upon our cooperation with grace. And so, the Spirit of the Christ-Child within us can starve and even languish and die.

The Blessed Virgin was chosen and fortified by God for the natural as well as the supernatural generation of the God-Man because God has made her so that she would not fail to cherish His gift to her. That is why she could say with confidence and with utter humility, "All generations shall call me Blessed, for He that is mighty hath done great things to me." (Luke 1:48). With her, it was the eternal Word in the flesh that was to make all generations call her Blessed. With us, each one in his own lifetime can *be*

blessed, if we will but honestly believe this great supernatural truth which Christ has taught us through our Church.
The words of Saint Elizabeth will become equally true for
us: "blessed art thou who hast believed, for the message of
the Lord to thee will be fulfilled." (Luke 1:45).

It is my earnest wish for you that you will take this doctrine at its face value and place yourself at the disposal of
Mary so that she may really and truly — "direct and order
all your doings in accordance with the will of her only Son."
Then truly will Christ be formed in you and, with Mary, you
will be constantly aware of that precious treasure within
you.

Then you will have no less incentive than Mary did, to set
aside every impulse of criticism of family or neighbor, every
impulse of selfishness, or pride, or unkind thoughts or words
or actions, or impatient acts of temper, even when provoked
beyond measure. You will plainly see the littleness of jealousy, or envy, or spite, or revenge, compared with the infinite bigness of your privilege of having Christ growing within
you; of having Him, you might say, "at your beck and call";
knowing that your every little movement to do what would
please Him or to stifle what would displease Him, is intimately noticed by Him.

Think how Mary's complete, all-out trust in God
prompted her to be silent even when Joseph momentarily
doubted her fidelity. Mary gave herself, body and soul, to
God when she said: "Be it done to me according to Thy
word." She gave her daily life, her every act, to Him, and
they were just acts of ordinary life, like ours, except that
there were probably many more aggravations and occasions
for humility. Suppose, for example, that you were approaching an isolated village on foot, as Mary did on the day they
arrived at Bethlehem, and suppose that the inn-keeper re-
fused to allow you to enter; could you easily imitate the
action of Mary? There are scores of occasions every day for
us to take ourselves in hand and do what we know Mary
would do, especially when we are always thinking of the
Infant Savior being formed in us.

God purposely made her life just as full of ordinary, every-day actions as our lives are, so that Christ being formed in us can give us the same incentive to do what Mary would do. We can do it with joy if we learn to put absolute trust in the Child within us. We can live our ordinary life, but live it giving it all to God — and we shall always have Mary to help us, yes, to do it for us, if we will simply make ourselves belong to her.

How strange, that most of us should find this so hard to do! We always seem to catch a little of the contagion of the "world" which will never "leave it to God." It takes real courage to leave it to God, especially when we see the tragedy that the world is making of its quest for happiness and peace. But constant reminders of Christ coming to birth in us can change our vision, can clinch our constant love for Him and make it reflect in all our acts. This giving all to God in everyday life is a greater source of grace than many penances and is truly living prayer.

It begets humility and makes us aware that even the best of us, who may be trying our best to act as Mary would, can often be exasperating to others. Love — active, thoughtful love, constant love, is the only cure for all our failures. When this love is centered on that Child-God within us and offered to Him by one who belongs to His Mother Mary, that one becomes the precious child of the Father; the apple of the Father's eye. He is then loved by the Father far more than he can ever hope to deserve or to respond.

Let us, then, hand over everything to Mary with a trust in her care which is very different from the trust of the world in riches. This trust of ours springs from the confidence in God's love — *come what may*. This trust is not concerned with health or wealth or wordly happiness, but it banks on the certainty that whatever God's Providence has in store for us comes to us from a loving all-wise Father. Christ in Gethsemani gave all to God in perfect love. His sorrow stemmed, not from fear, but from our perversity. Mary's "fiat" extended to the Cross. She alone saw her darling dead upon the Cross and still was able to trust the word of the

Father: "This is My beloved Son in whom I am well pleased." (Matt. 3:17). Let us, then, try to make Mary's thoughts and acts the pattern of our lives!

CHAPTER VII

IN GOD'S WAYS

Some years ago, I spent the month of July at a delightful vacation spot in the Adirondack Mountains in northern New York State. I was not, however, exactly "on vacation", even though the time spent was very interesting and enjoyable. On the contrary, I was engaged in intensive study at the Preachers Institute for teachers, preachers and missionaries, given by a staff of experts under the auspices of the Catholic University of America.

While there, I took copious notes during eighty-eight hours of instruction on Creative Thinking, Sermon Structure, Sermon Style, The Art Of Expression, etc. In addition, I listened to and criticized one hundred and twenty sermons. I also delivered and was criticized as to four sermons of my own composition.

But beyond all that, and almost as important, I lived in close association with forty other priests from all parts of the world. There were monks, friars, and religious priests representing twelve different religious orders, together with diocesan priests from twelve different cities.

When I returned to Westminster Abbey, I sat down and asked myself: What is the most valuable fruit of all this experience that I can share with the readers of my books? After consulting my notes and doing a lot of thinking, I concluded that the core of it all was summed up in one sentence taken from the life story of Saint Madeline Sophie Barat, Foundress of the Madames of the Sacred Heart. The book was given to me at the Mother House of the Madames at Albany, New York, when I was on my way home at the close of the Institute. The sentence in the book referred to the objective of the novices entering religious life, but I will remodel it a little and address it to each one who is reading this book:

> **"The most important work you can do is to learn the ways of God, and to understand yourself so that you can set yourself firmly in God's ways."**

Please do not conclude that this is a departure from the guidance of Mary recommended in the previous chapter. As a matter of fact, this sentence could most aptly be thought of as Mary's answer to the conclusion of the prayer which I have recommended to you: "By thy merits and most holy intercession do thou direct and order all my doings in accordance with the will of thine only Son."

Not only is it in accordance with the wish of Mary, but the Teaching Church definitely wants each one of you to know that, whatever else you may be doing in your daily life, all of it should be intended to enable you to "learn the ways of God", and equally important, "to understand yourself," really and truly and without self-deception, "so that you can set yourself firmly in God's ways." That means: Every moment of every day is an occasion to practice the principal purpose of your life, namely, Project Sainthood.

Perhaps you are beginning to get a hint of what I am leading up to. You should, indeed, because it is the same thing I have tried to refer to in every chapter of this last book of mine. It is that God invites every living soul to enter and practice the Way of Perfection, which is open to all and is not limited to those who devote themselves to God's service by leaving all things to follow Him. It is indeed the way in which God wishes all men and women to use this world in which He has placed us to find our way to heaven. And so, let us not be disappointed that a new look at the teaching of pastors and missionaries has not given us a brand new objective but rather, let us feel assured that we have been on the right track all the time.

The Catholic Faith is worth so much more to each one of us than we can realize, that even the greatest of saints is a pauper in the midst of plenty. An unrepentant sinner is simply unbelievably blind to the love of God.

The coin of the realm of our spiritual world is Sanctifying Grace which, as I have often reminded you, means Saint-Making Grace. It is available in infinite abundance to every one of us whether sick or well, rich or poor, crippled or sound, young or old, learned or unlearned. There is no limit to the *amount* any one can earn. There is no handicap to limit one person as compared with any other person. There is no such thing as "capitalist imperialism" to crowd out the little people in the harvest of grace. This is one field in which all men and women *are* created free and equal. But why is it, as the little boy said, that "some are so much more equal than others? "

That is the enigma that is the more puzzling the further one advances in Project Sainthood. The easy answer is that grace is a free gift from God and if God does not give it one simply does not receive it. But that is a misleading and evasive answer. It is true in one sense, but it must always be remembered that one's failure to receive grace is always coupled with a fault that is not from God.

As Saint Paul puts it: "We ask and exhort you in the Lord Jesus, that, as you have learned from us how you ought to live in pleasing God . . . so you would progress still more. . . . . For this is the will of God — your sanctification." (I. Thes. 4:1-3). So you see that while God wills your sanctification, He couples it with your progress in living so as to please God. And this is the same thing as what we have quoted from the story of Mother Barat, that your most important work is to learn the ways of God and to learn to understand yourself so that you can set yourself firmly in God's ways.

This, then, becomes the whole formula for placing yourself on the Way of Perfection, which is the way of God. Our text says that this is your *most important work*, but what I want most that you should understand is that it is not something that you should carry on as a special spiritual activity parallel to the work of living your life in the world. Quite the contrary, it means the way of doing everything that you do all the time. Of course, there are many helps that are purely spiritual in nature, but it is your every day life that is at issue.

The most obvious of these helps are daily Mass and Communion and weekly Confession. It is impossible to over estimate the value of these helps and impossible to spend the time which they require in a more profitable way. True, a mother of small children may seem to have duties which would make daily Mass impossible for a time. But even she would contrive to go fairly frequently if she fully realized the reward.

And certainly, weekly Confession is available to everyone. It is the strengthening grace of the Sacrament of Penance that makes weekly Confession one of the greatest helps in the Way of Perfection. Absolution blots out the past, but Sacramental Grace looks entirely to the future. No one who really understands the value of this grace would ever fail to take advantage of it.

While these helps pay greater dividends in Sanctifying Grace than any other way of spending time, they also help to make the rest of every day more profitable in the same commodity. This is the field where all of us have the greatest opportunity to improve the use of our time. Every minute of every day can be made an important part of Project Sainthood. The most profitable way of using all the time of every day is in prayer.

Now, please, I beg you, do not set me down as a dreamer suggesting the impossible, and then discount everything else that I wish to say. The concept of prayer has several quite specific meanings which might be quite inappropriate to my statement that prayer is the best way to fill all of the time which one does not spend in church. These specific applications of the meaning of prayer are all good. The more time one can spend at them the better. What I mean, however, by the prayer that can fill all of one's time, is a habit of mind that can be cultivated and improved throughout one's lifetime. It is the habit of relating every thought and word and act of one's life to God. Even the most trivial item then becomes important in God's eyes.

The best way to begin to cultivate this habit is to realize one important thing which is at the basis of all reality. It is this: Because of His infinity, God's relationship to each one of you is precisely the same as if you were the only soul for whom He made this world and this universe. His love for you is as if you were the only soul for whom He had allowed Himself to be crucified.

It is, of course, impossible for us to realize this idea fully and accurately because we have nothing else which even comes near to being comparable with it. No human love even approaches God's love for each one of us. And He has this love for us, even when we make ourselves His enemies and drive Him out of our souls by mortal sin. But, the very love He has for sinners makes sin an act of ingratitude that is as far beyond our capacity to appraise as His love is beyond our capacity to return.

To be sure, it is impossible for us to fully realize this truth because of our finiteness, but it is not by any means impossible for us to *know* it. Christ expressed it in many ways: "Are not two sparrows sold for a cent? And yet it is impossible for one of them to fall to the ground without your heavenly Father's will. And as for you, He takes every hair of your head into His reckoning. Do not be afraid, then; you count for more than a host of sparrows. (Matt. 10:29-31).

That does not mean that God counts the hairs of your head and keeps it in His memory. His knowledge is far more intimate than that, not only as to the hairs of your head, but as to the millions of cells of those hairs and each cell is as complicated as a battleship in its design. God's knowledge stems from His power of keeping every cell in existence. How unimportant is the knowledge of their number compared with the knowledge of their being which causes them to be!

The chief function of your body in this world is to make a dwelling place for your soul. The highest function of your soul, the thing that makes God call man His own image, is that capacity of the soul to know and to will and to love. Does all this make it any easier for you to know how close God is to you? If God is so intimately concerned with every movement of your will, does it not begin to be clear why your most important work is to learn the ways of God and to understand yourselves so that you can set yourselves firmly in God's ways? That is all it takes to enter and pursue Project Sainthood.

Thinking of God's intimate presence is the surest way to cultivate the habit of conforming ourselves to that Presence in everything we do. And that is all it takes to make us saints. The externals of saints lives and surroundings are no different from those of sinners. So, too, their experiences are similar to ours. Every state of life makes a perfect pattern into which conformity to God's ways leads to perfection.

The habit of conformity makes it apply to the busiest moments or the most trying moments of the life of each one of us. The bitter and the sweet, the unexpected and the planned, all resolve into perfection if God is the ever-present Partner of our thoughts and words and acts.

Children are sometimes good, sometimes bad, sometimes disobedient — perhaps quite sinfully so. Sometimes they would try the patience of Job. But God is in them just as He is in you. He has made you his instrument to deal with them either in your own way or in His way. His way is the saints way — the Way of Perfection.

Husbands are sometimes wonderful, sometimes cantankerous, perhaps even sinfully so. God has made husbands and wives as teams to bring each other and their children to heaven with a greater capital of grace than either would earn alone. God had provided the Sacramental Grace of the Sacrament of Marriage to make this possible or at least easier. God loves each member of every family more than any human being could possibly love any of them. Each member of the team should be willing to go not just half way, but *all* the way to make the team-work successful.

This involves sacrifice and constant work especially if only one of the team is willing to seek success in God's way. But, even the most difficult problem can become easy if God's intimacy with the success of the team be always kept in mind. If God's interest is kept constantly in mind, He will provide the means of overcoming every temptation to anger, retaliation, pouting, caustic replies. And in doing so He will heap up oceans of Sanctifying Grace to make crosses into treasures.

The people who enter our lives outside the family circle also provide gold-mines of grace. Some are close friends or relatives. Others are domestic or other employees, neighbors near and far, casual acquaintances, trades people, professional associates, social contacts, benefactors or beneficiaries of our charities, Catholics, anti-Catholics, saints and sinners. Some we love easily — others are ready to cheat and despise us. God is interested in our contact with each one of them. He loves them all, even the worst sinners. You are an instrument of God's Providence for each 'of them. They are instruments of God's Providence for you.

Perhaps they are permitted by God's Providence to try your patience, to tempt you to sin, to be objects of your charity, to be examples of virtue, to give scandal to be shunned. Every thought or word or act in relation to any of them is an occasion for you to set yourself firmly in God's ways!

For most of us, the very best way to make use of these occasions of grace is within our own souls. If we start immediately to cultivate the habit of stifling uncharitable or critical thoughts we will soon find ourselves getting away from that dangerous vice of comparing ourselves with others or comparing others with our ideas of what they should be.

This habit, once started, we will soon find ourselves being reminded in time to stifle the impluse to *say* something uncharitable, or critical, or caustic, or impatient, to others. And as *that* becomes a habit we will find ourselves more and more often urged to *do* only those things that reflect that constant mindfulness of God in our hearts. It will only then remain for us to turn all this into prayer, which it will be, when our motive for it all becomes firmly set in God's ways. We will begin each day with prayer for God's grace and, if possible assistance of Holy Mass, and fill it with adoration all day long, whatever may be the intensity of our worldly pursuits.

Please do not let yourself think that I am talking about Utopia — which would be nice to think about as worldly cares drop away toward the end of life. Nor is it something that might cause one to say: "Yes, that is a good idea – I will start practicing it right away." True, I wish with all my heart that you would begin this minute to wish to acquire these habits. They must, however, be approached with the knowledge that they constitute the Way of Perfection and cannot be won without firm determination and steadfast cooperation with the grace of God.

I am trying to practice what I am preaching. I can tell you from long experience that it is not easy, but it is worth more than all it costs. In fact, it is *the* most profitable way to spend one's time!

CHAPTER VIII

THE SACRED HEART OF JESUS AND CHRISTMAS

In Chapter Six we discussed the Advent of Christmas in the Heart of Mary. In Chapter Seven, we dwelt on the Foundation of Mary's love, the God-Man in our hearts. It is now fitting that we should advert to the source of all love found in that petition of the Litany of the Sacred Heart:

Heart of Jesus — formed by the Holy Spirit in the womb of the Virgin Mother — have mercy on us.

The true and perfect joy of Christmas shines with its greatest intensity when seen in the light of the Heart of Jesus springing from the Heart of Mary. This is true because there is no joy which can be compared with the joy of love. The paradox of the joy of love is that both the joy and the love are intensified when they are etched with pain.

One sometimes hears it said that the devotion to the Sacred Heart of Jesus and the Immaculate Heart of Mary is an innovation that was never thought of until it was invented as a result of the private revelations made by Our Lord Jesus Christ to Saint Margaret Mary Alacoque in the seventeenth century. This idea betrays a poverty in the sharing of the riches of the Bible story of the Incarnation. The Heart of Jesus and the Heart of Mary are of the essence of the Bible story of the Incarnation in its very beginning at the

Annunciation; in its manifestation at the Nativity and Epiphany; and in an ever more tender compassion at every stage of the childhood and young-manhood of Christ; reaching an infinite depth of divine and human charity at Gethsemane and Calvary.

And what does it mean to say that the Hearts of Jesus and Mary are of the essence of the story of the Incarnation? It means just this: the human heart, because it is the ever-active source of the life-blood of the body, is instinctively recognized as the energizing matrix of the soul with all its human faculties of knowing and willing and, above all, of loving and suffering. Mary's heart was the focal point between humanity and divinity when the Archangel Gabriel brought her that all-but-unbelievable message of love which made her the Mother of God. Mary's Heart responded in an ecstacy of love when she consented to receive Him on behalf of the human race. Mary's Heart generated the Heart of Jesus and made her Heart one with His.

The Incarnation in its entirety is an act of infinite love. It is, moreover, an act of wounded love. At its Annunciation it was an act of wounded divine love. Later, as Jesus became the object of coldness and rejection and finally of persecution and, last of all, of torture and death it became evident to us as wounded human love. Being God, however, the newly born Infant Jesus bore in His tiny Heart that wounded human love made infinite by the power of divine love from which it sprang.

Long before the days of the Incarnation, the Son of God used the lips of the Psalmist to announce Him and say: "Behold, I come. In the head of the book it is written of Me that I should do Thy will. To do Thy will, O My God, is all My desire, to carry out that law of Thine which is written in My Heart. (Ps. 39:8). The same sentiment moved His Heart then as moved His Heart in the Garden of Gethsemane: "Not My will, but Thine be done." (Matt. 26:40).

The creation of the world and of man by the Triune God might be called an act of purely divine love. God created man in His own image that man might be able to share in God's eternal happiness. But, from the very beginning until the present day and in all probability until the end of time, man's misuse of his capacity to know and love has been a wound in the Heart of God. And here let me repeat what I have said before; man's failure to appreciate God's love is truly a wound in the Heart of God, even though, within the divine nature, nothing can diminish the infinite beatitude of *being* God. And this is true even though man's frailty and infedelity might be called an essential characteristic of God's plan for this world.

Jesus Himself said that it was "necessary" that the Son of Man should suffer. (Luke 24:26); Why was it necessary? Because, as I have also said before, God intended this world to be a "vale of tears", since in no other way could man possibly come to know the depth of His love. What a different place heaven would be if God had simply created the elect, each in a state of perfection fit for heaven, and placed them in heaven without ever showing them to what length God was willing to go to win heaven for them. And, more important still, without ever giving them an opportunity to reflect that love in themselves by the faint imitation of it that is possible by the exercise of the supernatural virtue of Faith.

Even the human love in the Heart of God is beyond the capacity of the heart of man to fully comprehend, but how much less would we understand it if we had not seen its everlasting constancy in spite of those who reject it and spurn it and despise it — despise their Creator, their King, their Lover, their Savior. It gives us an inkling as to what our love means to Jesus when we see that He is willing to submit to the hate and insults and repudiation of those who cast themselves into hell. And He does this only to give us, and them, a sample of the love He has for us.

Only in heaven will we fully appreciate His love. We will appreciate it then, only because our experience in this world will have given us the capacity to truly appraise the immensity of the love which He has shown us by His Incarnation. True, we will fully appreciate it only in heaven, but even here, with half an eye of faith, we can appreciate enough to make us head-over-heels in love with God; head-over-heels keen to adore the Infant Savior; head-over-heels ready to give Him our hearts; to unite our hearts with His Sacred Heart.

The incentive for the extremity of our human love should be increased when we realize that He came in spite of our unanimous sharing in the wounding of His love. Each one of us, except the Blessed Virgin, is in some degree a Magdalen. Each of us, then, has a debt of gratitude that should immeasurably increase our love and our appreciation of His love.

Did I say "except the Blessed Virgin?" Does she, then, have less cause for love than we? In one sense that is true; she did not have the incentive of having been forgiven, to increase her love. *But* she has the far greater incentive of having been redeemed from the need of forgiveness. And, in addition, she has the incentive of having received fullness of grace. This gave her a perception of Christ's love that made her Heart one with the Heart of Jesus. Thus, she did not contribute to the wounding of His Heart, but rather she shared with Him the wounding of her Heart with the wounding of the Heart of God.

At the Incarnation, when Mary "pondered all these things in her Heart" she may be said to have been the "proxy" for the wounded Heart of the Infant Incarnate God. He, in His humanity at least, was too little to be concerned about the hatred and envy and jealousy which filled the heart of Herod, the puny king of the Jews, when he heard from the non-Jewish Magi, the news of the real King of the Jews, spelled with a capital "K".

The shepherds and the Angels and the Magi gave loving homage to the tiny God-King, but those who needed Him most — those who were indebted to Him for all that they had — those whom God the Father had favored with His love and special protection among all the people of the world — those who had the most to gain by His coming — not only failed to give him the loving homage that was His due, but, with hearts filled with malice and hate, sought to murder this helpless and innocent King of Love.

Indeed, the prophecy of holy Simeon to Mary was fulfilled long, long before the tragic ending of the life of her holy Child. The chill brutality of the murder of the innocent children of Bethlehem pierced her devoted Heart as did the coldness of those who remained aloof all His life long. Indeed, it was Mary's Heart of wounded love, together with the Heart of Saint Joseph, that almost alone gave consolation to the wounded Heart of God as she "pondered all these things in her Heart."

How significant are the words of Saint John at the opening of his Gospel: "He, through whom the world was made, was in the world and the world treated Him as a stranger. He came to what was His own, and they who were His own gave Him no welcome." (John 1:10-11). How utterly impossible it seems that the most precious event in all the history of the world, was acknowledged at its true worth by just two hearts together with the fleeting homage of a handful of shepherd boys. Nor can the sadness of this rejection be lessened by saying that His own did not *know* that He had come. It was the selfish turning away from God of almost the whole of His people that deprived them of the *grace* to know how to expect the coming of their Messiah. Most of His own had lost the art of love because they had lost the will to serve.

The Heart of Jesus, formed by the Holy Spirit in the womb of the Virgin Mother, had no need to wait until the year 1675 to be disclosed to Saint Margaret Mary as the wounded Heart of the King of Love pained by the coldness of most of those who needed Him, and grateful — yes, grateful for the consolation and reparation offered by the loving and compassionate Hearts of Mary and Joseph.

What a sad picture I am painting to dampen the ardor of our joy as we kneel with Mary and Joseph around the Crib at Bethlehem. By no means is it a sad picture! It is, however one that we should learn to understand as it was planned by God. Saint John again, will tell us why: "But all those who did welcome Him, He empowered to become the children of God, all those who believe in His Name; . . . through Jesus Christ grace came to the world, and truth. The only-begotten Son who abides in the bosom of the Father has Himself become our interpreter." (John 1:12-18).

There is the whole joyful message of the Incarnation! Not all will receive it; not all, at any time, have received the Word of God with welcome. All the Jews later heard the message from John the Baptist, but only a few really took it to heart. The reason? — they were not looking for the King of Love. They were only interested in a King who would further their political interests and give them power over their enemies.

The number of His own who gave Him no welcome was indeed great, but their number is of far less importance than the number of those who did welcome Him, few though they were at first, and few in comparison always. Their joy at Christmas is ever greater because the little King of Love allowed Himself to really *need* their love, their consolation, their reparation for the coldness of the multitude. And, in giving this loving consolation and welcome to the tiny King of Glory their love is immensely increased by the fact that it is needed and desired and welcomed by Him for whom they are given the power to become the children of God.

However great may be the number of those who have treated Him as a stranger, it is for those who are empowered to become the children of God that heaven was made. It is they whose names are written in the Book-of-Life or, as we now know, it is they whose names *may* be written in the Heart of Jesus. And so it is whenever we approach the Christmas season today. The Heart of that innocent Infant needs consolation as perhaps never before. Certainly the number of those to whom He is a stranger is greater than ever before. That, however, need not lessen our joy that we have been given the grace to welcome Him. In fact, in a sense, it can be an occasion of greater joy because it is a challenge to our love. Those whose names are written in the Heart of Jesus are loved by Him, each with a divine and human love beyond the capacity of any human love to return and beyond our capacity to understand. It is as if the world and heaven had been made for each one of them alone.

But also, those whose names are not yet written in His Heart, are loved by Him and sought by Him with the same longing that He expressed for the "rich young man" whom

He invited to follow Him. This young man had, as he said, kept all the Commandments from his youth, but he remained aloof from the Savior because his love for earthly treasure made him blind to the incomparable value of treasure in heaven. And yet, we are told that, "Jesus loved him, and said to him, 'One thing thou lackest. Go, sell whatever thou hast, and give to the poor, and thou shalt possess treasure in heaven; and come, follow Me,' " (Mark 10:21).

Christ's love for all of them, or, I should say, each of them is the same today. Being God, His interest in every soul is as if that soul were the only one for whom His Incarnation was planned. Yet, each one of the millions of our neighbors who lead good lives, who have kept the Commandments from their youth, who feed the poor and give shelter to the fatherless, each one of them may be a wound in the Heart of Jesus because "one thing is lacking." They do not wholeheartedly give themselves to Christ. They hold back some part of their love because of human respect or selfish unwillingness to trust the promise of Christ that they are safe when they hear those whom He has sent to teach them.

As long as they live, Christ loves them and invites them to His Heart and to His Sacraments, especially the Blessed Sacrament of His love. They remain aloof for reasons of their own, not for reasons that they have learned from Him. The consolation that Christ asks of us is on their account. He loves them; He offers them His love; but he deigns to use our help, nay, to say that He *needs* our help to win them. "Look" He says, "I tell you! raise your eyes and survey the fields; for they are already white for harvesting. The reaper receives wages and gathers a harvest for eternal life, so that both the sower and the reaper may rejoice together." (John 4:35-36).

Jesus Himself is the "sower" of grace. He invites each one of us to reap a harvest for eternal life by helping the grace He offers to bear fruit in the souls of those who are well-disposed and yet remain aloof from the Heart of Him who is the King of Love. This grace of the divine Sower is especially abundant during the Christmas season which is the manifestation of His divine love bursting the bounds of eternity and budding into time in the Heart of the Infant Savior and cherished in the spotless human Heart of Mary. The love of the Sacred Heart of Jesus is by all odds the choicest Christmas present we can receive in this world. And, as our Savior tells us, it is one that we can also help to give.

Saint Matthew tells us of our Savior's desires in regard to the millions who do not know Him as He wishes to be known: "And observing the multitudes He felt compassion for them because they were harassed and scattered like sheep that have no shepherd. Then He said to His disciples, 'The harvest is plentiful, but the laborers are few. Pray, therefore, the Master of the Harvest to send out laborers into His harvest.'" (Matt. 9:36-38).

We used to hear this same quotation voiced after every Benediction with the Blessed Sacrament as a plea for vocations to the priesthood and religious life and, indeed, it is. But in its context here it is equally an invitation to each one of us to every Catholic to change the atmosphere of the celebration of Christmas from the pagan orgy to which materialism is directing it in our land, back into the intensely personal presentation of the living God into the heart of every human being in the world.

During this eighth decade of the twentieth century the Christ Child is inviting all of us to go forth into the harvest which He has prepared as never before, perhaps, in the history of the world. Our late beloved Holy Father, Pope John XXIII convinced the world, as never before, of the love of Christ for all men without exception, as exemplified in his own person as Christ's Vicar. And now, with that leaven of love pervading the world, Pope John's prayer for the Second Vatican Council is being copiously answered. The Divine Spirit sent by the Father in the Name of Jesus, Who dost infallibly assist and guide the Church — is indeed pouring forth His gifts upon the works of the Council, and through it, upon the whole world.

But these gifts, however pregnant of love, will only reach the hearts of those who are "harassed and scattered like sheep that have no shepherd," if we, each one of us, does his or her part to help them to reach their intended goal.

And how should we do this? By becoming more fervent and more out-going as Catholics. I have said that our late Holy Father, Pope John XXIII, has convinced the world as never before, of the love of Christ. I should have said, Christ has used the precious example of our late Holy Father to convince the world of *His* love. He now asks you to let Him use your heart to extend the example of Pope John to convince all of those who have even the remotest contact with your life. You can answer His request in almost everything you do and say. There is not even a great saint who could not have been at least a little more fervent in spreading the love of Christ. There is not a fallen-away Catholic who is not the object of the wounded love of the Heart of Jesus as long as life lasts. There is not a single Catholic whose actions are not important to the Heart of Christ.

The actions and words of the lax and fallen-away Catholics are *the* greatest obstacles to Christian reunion! They keep more people away from the Church than Communism ever will. Furthermore, those who do these harmful acts and say these harmful words have hearts more vulnerable to recovery than do the Communists — not by threats or scolding or argument, but by kindness and, above all, by your good example, and by your prayers in their behalf. If you are determined to saturate yourself and your dear ones with the notion that you and they are important as apostles of the Sacred Heart of Jesus, you can do much to help to accomplish the results hoped for from the Second Vatican Council by Pope John and Pope Paul VI.

There is no better way to start this apostleship than by having the image of the Sacred Heart enthroned in your home or, if you have already done this, by increasing your attention to that devotion which Christ has promised will bring you all the graces needed to do for Him what He wishes you to do. This is particularly important in North America where human respect holds so many Catholics back from being what the hagiographer would call *true* "confessors" of their faith. That means one who, with true love and confidence and trust in the love of the Sacred Heart, strives mightily by kindness, by good example, and by zeal to show the well-intentioned as well as the ill-intentioned neighbor the pity of the ignorance that separates them from the blessings of the Catholic Faith.

This decade of the twentieth century is perhaps the most propitious time in all the history of the Church to turn the tide of thinking among those who are "harassed and scattered like sheep that have no shepherd." You may think that their scoffing indifference is invulnerable to anything you could do to help them, and so it would be if you were acting alone, but if you are acting as an instrument of the Sacred Heart, never forget that He has promised to "shower down blessings on all your undertakings." (Promise No. 5).

It is with a little chuckle of spiritual delight that I have accepted as my own, the following prayer to be recited every evening. It is reported that a Poor Clare Nun who had just died, appeared to her Abbess who was praying for her, and said to her: "I went straight to heaven, for, by means of this prayer, recited every evening, I paid all my debts." And this is the prayer:

> **"Eternal Father, I offer Thee the Sacred Heart of Jesus, with all Its love, all Its suffering and all Its merits. First, to expiate all the sins I have committed this day and during all my life. Glory be to the Father, and to the Son, and to the Holy Spirit; as it was in the beginning, is now, and ever shall be; world without end. Amen. Second, to purify the good I have done badly this day and during all my life. Gloria Patri ... Third, to supply for the good I ought to have done that I have neglected this day and during all my life. Gloria Patri. ..."**

Let us try to behave so that this prayer will not remind us of too many things done badly or neglected! And so that the Heart of the Infant Jesus formed in the Heart of Mary will abide with us at Christmas and always!

CHAPTER IX

THE SACRED HEART AT HOME

The subject which I wish to discuss in this chapter is concerned with the Ninth Promise made by Our Lord Jesus Christ to Saint Margaret Mary Alacoque in favor of those devoted to His Sacred Heart. It reads as follows: *I Will Bless the Homes in Which the Picture of My Sacred Heart Shall Be Exposed and Honored.*

I have searched the New Testament in vain for texts which would be appropriate for this subject. This fruitless search, however, has taught me what I should have realized long before. During the lifetime of Christ upon earth, His love was expressed in almost constant public works and teaching. There are, of course, hints of the intimate expressions of love in the homes in which He visited and lived, especially in Nazareth and the home of Mary and Martha and Lazarus in Bethany.

There is constant evidence, too, of the wounding of His love in the unbelievable affronts and insults which He received. But these were all addressed to His person while He was there present and it was only gradually and later that His love and His sorrows and the intimacy of His relationship to us was associated with His Heart.

In fact, it was only at the very end of His life that His Heart was opened to pour forth the Blood and Water of atonement and cleansing which are now represented by an outpouring of rays of light which Christ described as He showed them to Saint Margaret Mary and said: "These rays represent the blood and water which gushed forth from the depth of My Mercy when My agonizing Heart was opened on the Cross. The pale rays symbolize the water which justifies the soul; and the red rays represent the blood, which is the life of the soul. These rays shield the soul before the wrath of My Father. Fortunate is he who lives in their brilliance, for the just hand of God will never reach him."

The blessed intimacy of the protection of life within the Heart of Jesus was less evident while the tragedy of it was being enacted. And so it is not surprising that the sacred writers who recorded these events many years after they happened, were chiefly concerned with passing on to future generations an account which would give certainty to the otherwise unbelievable reality of a crucified God. The goings-on within men's hearts and within men's homes were the *result* of their stories and letters rather than the *substance* of them.

Saint John who wrote his Epistles, perhaps, last of all, comes the nearest to expressing the individual's reaction to the love story, the tragic love story, which brought the Heart of God into the hearts of men. The last words of Saint John's first Epistle give the strongest hint of the beginnings of the abode of Christ's Heart in the homes of men. He wrote:

> "The man who has been born of God, we may be sure, keeps clear of sin; that divine origin protects him, and the evil one cannot touch him. And we can be sure that we are God's children, though the whole world about us lies in the power of the evil one. We can be sure, too, that the Son of God has come to us, and has given us a sense of truth; we were to recognize the true God, and to live in His true Son. He is true God and eternal life. Beware, little children, of false gods." (I. John 5:19-21).

The evil one to whom Saint John refers came into furious combat with Christ in Person and fought His conquest of hearts all His life long until the bitter ending which, in the apparent total victory of Satan, in reality marked his everlasting defeat. But in the mysterious Providence of God, the

defeat of Satan at the Crucifixion did not extinguish the
power of Satan, but rather established an absolutely safe refuge from his power which men could learn to use or could,
through their own fault, stray away from and risk everlasting
destruction at the hand of Satan and his evil agents among
men.

Saint John's Epistles as well as his Gospel sound the
pleading call of Christ's love more than any other part of
public revelation. In fact, it was only because the ringing
truth of the call and the deadly danger in the warning were
becoming dimmed and forgotten that they were renewed by
Christ and crystallized into definite promises which offered
men the means of tying their hearts within the safe refuge
of the Heart of God. Those who ignored the pleading of
Christ Himself laid themselves wide open to the specious
guile of Satan and became the Antichrists of Saint John's
day.

Satan's tactics have never varied and God has continued
to allow them to entrap those who will not listen to the call
of His Heart. They are legion today and they are just as evil
and just as smooth as they have ever been. And here is the
point to remember: they do most of their work on other
days than Sunday. True, they are on hand and watchful during Mass on Sunday and around the doors of the church, but
that is only because they are determined not to miss a single
opportunity. Their throughgoing professional seduction, however, is hammering away on week-days, on the street, at
work, on the air waves, on the news stand, at the theater, on
the beaches, everywhere. But without any doubt, the citadel
which they eye with sharpest envy is the place of abode of
each and every one of you.

Whether you live alone or with one companion or belong
to a large family or a community like mine, it is in your
home that the safety of your soul is fortified or else en-
dangered. Week-day Mass in our churches used to be followed by the prayer to Saint Michael Archangel to defend us
in battle; to be our safeguard against the malice and snares
of the Devil; to thrust down into hell Satan and the other
evil spirits who roam through the world seeking the ruin of

souls. No doubt this prayer was useful and efficacious, but the one which followed it — the three-fold plea for mercy from the Sacred Heart of Jesus was the prayer that sent us out into the street reminded of the surest protection of all — the indwelling presence of His Sacred Heart which is available to us in proportion to the intimacy of love which we have enabled Him to establish in our heart.

God is present to us in many different ways which differ from each other in their operation. His power is necessary at every moment to keep us in natural existence. Natural existence, however, avails little unless He is also present in sanctifying Grace which supernaturalizes the soul and plants in it the seed of glory. God is also substantially present to us in a new way as often as we receive Holy Communion. He is present, too, in the thread of His Providence which sweetly orders every moment of every experience of our lives. He is present in the grace of every other Sacrament as well.

But the presence which sweetens and strengthens and makes lasting the blessings of the Holy Eucharist is that presence of His Sacred Heart which is truly a different way and brings with it an intimacy and a confidence which exceeds every other grace. It is the presence of His Sacred Heart in the home and in each member of the family that not only fortifies it as a stronghold impregnable to the forces of evil, but makes it a power-house of grace to send its members safely out into the world as intruments of His love to benefit all who will share that love with them.

How do I know all this? It is implied in the Deposit of Faith, in the words of Christ at the Last Supper, and in the text of Saint John's Epistle which I have quoted. It is made doubly certain by the promises made to Saint Margaret Mary and proved by the miracles of grace which have followed in its train. "I will bless the homes in which the picture of My Sacred Heart shall be exposed and honored." "I will give them all the graces necessary for their state of life." "I will establish peace in their families. — I will console them in all their difficulties — I will be their secure refuge during life and more especially at the hour of death. — I will shower down abundant blessings on all their undertakings. — Sinners shall find in My Heart a Source and boundless ocean of mercy. — Tepid souls shall become fervent. — Fervent souls shall rise speedily to great perfection. — Persons who propagate this devotion shall have their names written in My Heart, and they shall never be effaced therefrom."

Even if these promises of Christ reported by Saint Margaret Mary were, at their origin, from a figment of her imagination, the obvious fruits and graces which have been showered on the world during the three centuries of their acceptance, would prove beyond the shadow of a doubt that they were honored and intended by the Sacred Heart Himself.

Some of you may have responded to this invitation and are praticing active devotion to the Sacred Heart enthroned in your homes. Some of you may cherish the thought that such a practice is too conspicuous and that it would have the opposite effect of antagonizing visitors or, perhaps, even some members of the family. Those in families of mixed marriage or whose dear ones are in families of mixed marriage are particularly vulnerable to that thought. And, since many of you fall in that class, either for yourselves or for very dear relatives or friends, I want to assure you with certainty that to cherish such a notion is to doubt the sincerity or the power of the Sacred Heart of Jesus who made the promises.

One reason that His promises are so prodigal is to bring a real challenge to our faith. Christ did not say: "If the picture of My Sacred Heart is accepted by everyone in the home and all the visitors, I will bless the house." All of His promises are unequivocal and definite and will be honored by Him. In turn, He wants true faith and trust in His promises without any reservations. Such faith begets love; such love begets courage; such courage begets action, prudent action, but fearless action, because it knows that it is backed by the power of the love in the Sacred Heart of Jesus.

Father Matheo Crowley-Boevey, the great apostle of enthronement of the Sacred Heart in homes, cites many victories achieved by this conquest of trusting love. One in particular, relates to mixed marriage. A very loving Catholic

mother prayed and wept a good deal over the tartly unsym-
pathetic attitude of her non-Catholic husband. An inspiration
came to her, however, as her two little girls were scheming
with their father in preparation for her birthday. She asked
her husband to give for her present that year his permission
to enthrone the Sacred Heart in the place of honor in their
living-room. It was, indeed, almost a miracle that he did consent, but he was determined not to be present for the little
ceremony of enthronement at which the little girls and their
mother prayed most earnestly for his conversion.

After it was over, however, the father came into the room
through curiosity and glanced at the picture, but lowered his
eyes under the loving beseeching glance of the Savior. He
was ashamed of his cowardice and looked again as if drawn
by some invisible power. That same quiet longing look still
pursued him, troubled him, exasperated him. He called to his
wife: "Whom have you brought into this house? There is
someone here! I tell you there is someone here." The
mother trembling with emotion called the little girls and had
them repeat the prayer they had a few minutes before recited for his conversion. This proof of confident loving faith
conquered him and, falling on his knees he clasped them to
his heart and rejoiced with them.

Perhaps your thought is: "It would be most unwise to try
that idea in my family, Father. You don't know my husband
— or my son-in-law — or my daughter-in-law." Yes, of
course, your situation *is* different, but it is the same Sacred
Heart, the same love, the same promises. There are no exceptions mentioned in the promises made by Jesus who is the
God of love. The only requirement is that you allow His
love to penetrate and drive away any timidity that you may
have that would cause you to hesitate to give His love a free
hand.

I am not asking that you become street preachers; I am
not asking you do to battle with difficult non-Catholic members of your family or acquaintance, but I do hope that each
one of you will try to do something more than you are
doing to promote devotion to the Sacred Heart in your own
home as well as in the homes of those dear to you. And, if

any of those homes do include difficult non-Catholics, they are not excepted.

Enthronement of the Sacred Heart is not an argumentative procedure. If it were I would never recommend it to you. I was a difficult non-Catholic husband too long to have any use for argumentative procedure. Not only is the enthronement non-argumentative, but, when entered into and practiced whole-heartedly, it is just the opposite of argumentative; it is giving Jesus Himself an opportunity to take command and express His love in a manner which He, God, has endowed with supernatural grace-giving powers.

Enthronement is not something complicated or difficult to accomplish. The essential is that a good picture or image of the Sacred Heart be installed in a prominent place in the principal room of the home and that, if at all possible, a priest be asked to come and bless it and lead an act of consecration of the family to the Sacred Heart. There is an official form of this act of consecration which may be used with or without the presence of a priest. The ideal procedure is to inscribe this act of consecration on a parchment or sheet or vellum paper and have it signed by all members of the family and kept near the enthroned Sacred Heart. When this is done it invites and makes easy the continued devotion to the Sacred Heart as a daily family affair.

I do hope that you will not hesitate to start this devotion because of the fear that it will be a burden to continue it or with the notion that Jesus will blame you less for not starting than He would for starting it and not being faithful to it. If it were "just another devotion" I would be the last one in the world to recommend it. It is by no means just another devotion. It is the very next thing to having the Blessed Sacrament in your home as was possible in the very early Church when families were budding martyrs.

This is not something that someone has thought up to try to regain weekday recognition of our Faith. It has a twofold special merit placed in it by Christ Himself. First, it is an ever present source of grace which is only exceeded by the Mass and the Sacraments themselves to which it invites and encourages every member of the family. Second, and equally important, it offers a privilege of consoling God, of making reparation to Him for our own neglect and for the appalling neglect and indifference and sacrilegious behavior of the world at large. This is not only a treasure house of merit, but it guarantees peace of soul which is beyond belief until you have really given it a trial.

It can re-make and re-perfect your family life, no matter how perfect it has been in the past. Its unifying effect on the family is probably more needed today than ever before in the history of Christianity. The mad scramble of automation, mass production, and organization has tended to place each member of a family in a different category, each with his own individual time-schedule, individual interests, individual associates, individual projects. None of these promote family love, family unity, family loyalty, or individual spirituality. The family devotion to the Sacred Heart tends to reverse all of these desintegrating forces. These forces have come to stay. We can never expect to eliminate them, but unless we strive earnestly to offset them we are making them penalties instead of blessings.

The advantage of this devotion is that when properly understood and properly practiced it becomes an underlying conditioner of everything we do. It makes the staying-together of praying-together into a cement that pervades all the actions of every member of the family which has its effects all day long, not just during the time of prayer. The greatest benefit of all is that it comes about that you will soon begin to see the hand of God for what it is, the intimate loving Father and Protector and Sanctifier of every member of the family. Whatever may happen — even the greatest tragedies — will be met with that peace of soul which springs from utter confidence that the Sacred Heart means it when He says that He will be your secure refuge during life.

Devotion begins to have its effects in individual souls. It makes them more docile, more lovable, more live-withable, but it is immensely more potent in its combined individual effects within a family and from the family it becomes an affair of the entire Church and from there it is an affair of tremendous importance to the entire world. If the Sacred Heart were to be enthroned in every Catholic family and this devotion were continued day-by-day it would, without a doubt, remake the world.

There is a fundamental contrast between the true Catholic motive for faith and that of the vast majority of those around us. The Catholic motive is really nothing less than an insight through the veil of the senses into the supernatural world where God is intimately close to each one of us. The motive for most of our neighbors stops at the limits of the senses and the conclusions of human reason drawn from them. Blessed with the true motive for faith, however, we may cut through all of the obstacles with which fallen man and the blighted material world have complicated our quest for God, and see Him as the immediate and sufficient loving Guide and Protector in every situation, even the greatest trials and crosses.

This motive suffices for all the answers and in every walk of life and every degree of education or no education at all. If suffices because, when God is known to be close at hand, He does supply every need and His love softens every trial. It causes one to live in God truly in the supernatural world and only incidentally in the material world where we may earn our way to heaven. It is this true motive for Catholic faith that is generated by the enthronement of the Sacred Heart in one's own home. This enthronement ushers the family into Christ's Kingdom which is not of this world and is not disturbed by the evils of this world however much our daily life may have to contend with them.

On Christ's side, the intimacy of His presence and the depth of His love is constant and perfect for every soul. On our side, however, the appreciation and reflection of that intimacy and love is the work of our lifetime. Even though the true Catholic motive for faith takes us spiritually past the veil of our senses and places us confidently close to God, the depth of that faith and the ardor of that love are the product of our constant effort to cooperate with grace and exercise that love.

The Catholic who is lukewarm or who has fallen away has, by neglecting that grace and failing in love, allowed the Catholic motive for faith to die and has fallen into the plight of those for whom the treasure of Sanctifying Grace hangs by a thread or not at all, because they are blinded by the sophistication of science and the world.

We will never know in this world the state of the souls of those who deny the Catholic Faith. We do know that it is possible for them to possess Sanctifying Grace, through the merciful Providence of God which extends to those who are baptized by water or by desire. The saving power of the Church applies to them if they are innocent of fault for their failure to follow the true way marked out by Christ. But we also know, as our beloved Holy Father, Pope Pius XII, told us in his encyclical on the Mystical Body of Christ, that their plight is unsafe and that they are a constant source of sadness to our Savior.

Christ wishes each one of us, priests, religious, and lay persons to be apostles to bring the knowledge of the love of His Sacred Heart to them and thus encourage them to come back into the safety of the Sacrament of His love. In doing this we immeasurably strengthen our own individual love for Him and build up within ourselves the riches of Sanctifying Grace which will make us true lovers of His Heart.

All honor given to the Sacred Heart starts from the tabernacle. By enthroning Him in our hearts at Holy Communion, we can enrich His enthronement in our homes and from there, hour after hour, our influence will go out into the hostile world and as His instrument of love we will help to draw countless souls to the tabernacle for the fulfillment of His prayer that they all may be one. Let us proclaim again to them and to ourselves the loving admonition of Saint John which I have quoted before: "We can be sure, too, that the Son of God has come to us and has given us a sense of truth. He is true God and eternal life. (I. John 5:20).

CHAPTER X

THE SACRED HEART
AND INFALLIBLE TRUTH

It is impossible to give sincere honest thought to the
Bible story of the Incarnation and the Mission of the Son of
God, without admitting the exact truth of the tremendous
conclusion of Saint Paul's great eulogy of the theological
virtue of Charity:

> **For now we see through a glass in a dark manner: But then
> face to face. Now I know in part: but then I shall know
> even as I am known. And now abideth Faith, Hope, and
> Charity, these three: but the greatest of these is Charity."
> (I. Cor. 13:12-130).**

Since the Word became flesh and dwelt among us there
can be no doubt but that the be-all and end-all of the relationship between God and man — between Jesus and each
individual soul — is *Love*. It is not just love as we understand human love in this world — not even the most exalted
relationship of self-giving between soul and soul. It is a benevolence of the Living God which is utterly incomprehensible
to a finite soul. But the more nearly it is understood, the
more completely does it absorb our capacity to reflect it in
a Christ-centered pattern of life.

Every episode in the life of Christ recounted in the Gospels shouts to us in an ever-obvious crescendo that nothing
but love — human love made infinite by divine love —

prompted the Son of God in everything He did; every thought and word and act of His whole life. The expression of this love was, first and always, to do the will of God the Father — but the will of God the Father was and is, to do what it takes to offset and atone for the evil ingratitude of the creature for whom the world was made — each individual man.

That, too, was the sole incentive — the all but unbelievable incentive — which inspired the Second Person of the Blessed Trinity to leave His heavenly home in the bosom of the Father and take our human nature; to give glory to the Father by restoring fallen man to His love. This He did by showing them a greater love than men could ever hope to return. "Behold, I come to do Thy will, O My God! " (Ps. 39:8). One cannot read the Gospel and find any other motive — the good of man — the salvation of man — heaven for man — for the love of God.

If it was so utterly obvious, why did it meet, for the most part, with suspicion and hate and persecution ending in torture and death? If it is now so utterly obvious, why does it still meet, for the most part, with suspicion and hate and persecution that takes almost every form from prohibition of its mention in our schools up to torture and death? That is, indeed, a difficult question to answer. But, in order to protect ourselves and our dear ones from the misunderstanding of those who form that "most part", we *must* find an answer.

Not only must we find an answer, but we must find an *infallible* answer so as to clinch our confidence in God and assure for us and our dear ones the fruit of God's love which is the purpose of our being in this world. And it is the purpose of this chapter to find that infallible answer.

The reason that I put it that particular way is that I want to discuss with you some of the ideas contained in a book which greatly assisted my own search for the faith and which I have used to help others many times since I first read it. The title of the book is: *CHRISTIANITY AND INFALLIBILITY — BOTH OR NEITHER.* That is indeed a rather severe-sounding title and seems rather far removed from Saint Paul's eulogy of Charity which I have quoted, and my insistence that love — Incarnate *Love*, is of the essence of our Faith. But I hope to show that it is not as far removed as it may appear at first sight.

One reason for the conformity of the two ideas is that the necessity for infallibility of a religion founded by and presently sponsored by God, is just as obvious as is the necessity for a total basis of love as the reason for any religion where God is concerned. The primary reason that the necessity of infallibility should be obvious is simple in the extreme. It is this: The idea of God and the idea of *fallibility* are contradictory terms; religion sponsored by God cannot, then, be fallible. But Christianity *is* the religion sponsored by God. To make this fact absolutely certain it was necessary that God should bring the proof within the realm of our sense knowledge. This He did by spending a short lifetime on earth as the God-Man, Jesus of Nazareth.

If Christianity, then, is the religion established and guaranteed by God, it must be protected by infallibility. Why, then, is it necessary to write a three-hundred-page book to answer this question more forcefully? The reason for the book and the reason for this chapter is to find out why two such obvious things as the love of God and His infallible protection of His Church are so far from obvious to a large majority of the world's people.

It might be thought that the mere suggestion of the existence of an infallible teaching authority would make it considered such a precious treasure that everyone, upon hearing of it, would examine the evidence with such a keen desire to find it acceptable that they would be in danger of overlooking what might be really valid objections. In fact, it was with such a desire that I, as an ardent Episcopalian, began taking instructions from a Catholic priest forty-odd years ago. Fortuantely, too, he was a humble priest, because I expressed my desire with very little tact. "I don't think it is possible that I will ever be a Catholic," I said, "but the claims of the Catholic Church are so prodigious that I think it would be foolish if I did not examine the evidence."

I have long ago discovered, however, that such a notion is not a common one. On the contrary, a recent conversation with a Protestant of very good-will indicates almost the opposite as the common view. I was talking with him about the possibility of the reunion of Christendom as a result of the goodwill which has been nourished by the charity of Pope John XXIII and the Second Vatican Council. I ventured the opinion that the greatest obstacle to reunion at the present time is the fact that it is not easy to be a good practicing Catholic so people have no incentive to examine the evidence. My friend surprised me by saying that he thought that the Catholic Church's claim of infallibility is the greatest obstacle to reunion.

Whether or not his estimate is correct, it points up the importance of the obligation of every Catholic to understand as fully as he possibly can the bed-rock truth behind the maxim: "Christianity and Infallibility — Both or Neither." It is important for two reasons; first, while love is the greatest of the virtues and the key to salvation, love is the flower of faith and must be anchored in a faith which, while admittedly a free gift from God, stems from a confidence in God which is proof against doubt, come what may. The second reason why it is important for every Catholic to understand the truth behind this maxim, is that unless he understands it thoroughly, he will be a hindrance rather than a help to every non-Catholic who might otherwise be led by his example.

In these last years of the twentieth century the importance of this understanding has increased immensely. There have been so many hateful things done within the Church and so much quenching of reverence in the changes that have been made that it has caused many to fall away with the notion that infallible protection of the Faith has ceased.

This has been immensely aggravated by two types of attack upon the *meaning* of infallibility. Ironically, these attacks stem from two directly opposite motives. One questions infallible direction as to the laws of moral behavior in order to justify, for example, contraception and abortion. The other questions it in order to demand rescinding of the

new liturgical Ordo and a return to a Tridentine interpretation of tradition. Both use the utterly vicious cliche' with
respect to papal documents of direction, "It's not infallible"
and continue, "so it's only a matter of opinion which, in
this case, happens to be wrong."

This amounts to a claim that the promise of Christ that
He would protect His Church from teaching error applies
only to that bare skeleton of the items of doctrine formally
declared to be irreformable in their dictation, and substitutes
the false notion that there is no obligation in conscience to
obey the directives of the Church's Magisterium if one
chooses to disagree.

This is not, and never has been the teaching of the
Church. The only difference between the absolutely binding
authority of the "*Ex Cathedra*" declarations and those of
the "Ordinary Teaching Authority" is that, if a theologian
has reason to believe that there is error or misunderstanding
in the latter type of declaration, he has an obligation to present his question to the Holy See and be prepared to accept
the decision as final. Any other interpretation of the status
of the Teaching Authority of the Catholic Church with respect to Faith, Worship or Moral Behavior would deny the
Promises of Christ and would place the Church of Rome in
exactly the same status as all the sects and schisms that have
sought to destroy the Bark of Peter since its beginning.

Every one of the sects and schisms down the centuries
which have resulted in disunion, has stemmed from refusal
to accept the directives of the Teaching Authority or refusal
to recognize that Teaching Authority as the final arbiter in
cases of disagreement.

This is not to say that there have never been justifiable
causes for dissatisfaction within the Church. Neither does it
affirm that there have never been grave offenders and sinners
among the popes. But the reason that the Church has sur-
vived until today is that the infinite wisdom and power of
the Holy Spirit dwelling in the Church *has* fulfilled the
Promises of Christ and preserved the integrity of the Deposit
of Faith and the code of moral behavior and worship. To

profess loyalty to the Holy See and then refuse obedience to the Holy Father because one disagrees with his directives and justifies the disobedience on the ground that the directive, "is not infallible," is to act directly contrary to the expressed will of Christ.

Unless all this is true, the Catholic Church has been hopelessly abandoned by the Holy Spirit and the Promises of Christ are meaningless. And that is equivalent to using the words of Saint Paul and saying: "We are of all men most pitiable." (I. Cor. 15:19).

It is to be hoped, then, that this digression has helped the Catholic reader to understand the importance of the truth behind the maxim contained in the title of the book, *CHRISTIANITY AND INFALLIBILITY — BOTH OR NEITHER*. My own response to the necessity of this maxim stems not only from my experience in trying to help non-Catholic inquirers, but also from my memory of my own reactions when I was a rather obstinate, or perhaps even obtuse non-Catholic myself. Let me try to explain why this is true. First, in order to be a non-Catholic Christian, one must believe that the Catholic Church, which for a long time was the only Christian Church, gradually began to teach error. This is proved for them by the fact of the "Reformation". They conclude that it would not have happened if it had not been necessary.

The only course left, then, if one accepts this as proof and still wishes to be a Christian, is to use his God-given reason to examine the Bible and the Churches claiming to be Christian and decide how he can best satisfy his desire to worship God. For most of them the course of least resistance is to continue in whatever sect they have been brought up and taught from childhood until something better is made to appeal to their reason or to their affection.

To them the claim of any church to be guided by an infallible teacher is the same thing as claiming magic. To them it seems like a frantic last-stand gesture to save the dwindling power of the hierarchy over the people. To many of them, moreover, it is something far more sinister. These regard the claim of infallibility as a crafty device of the Catholic hierarchy to stop up the eyes and ears of the faithful against the friendly approaches of those more enlightened Protestant Christians who would otherwise gladly show them the error of their way.

Lest you should think that I am exaggerating the picture, I will quote verbatim from a letter addressed to me by a woman who sincerely wishes to be a good believer in Christ. She says: "There are many things in the Roman Church that attract me to it, but the unbending attitude of being completely right and brooking no disagreement with its teachings is intolerance of the worst kind and far from a Christian attitude." Of course, the scope of the infallibility claimed by our Teaching Authority is not precisely a claim to be "completely right", but it is very obvious that it is, in principle, *the* great obstacle which stands between this good woman and any consideration of the deposit of faith which the gift of infallibility was designed to protect.

So, when all is said and done, it should be quite easy for us to see that the notion that it would be impossible for Christianity to perdure into the twentieth century without an infallible Teaching Authority, far from being obvious to the non-Catholic Christian, usually strikes him as so preposterous that he does not even care to examine the evidence. A little thought, however, should enable us to see the reason for this extreme divergence of viewpoint. The Catholic either takes it for granted or quickly sees the obvious necessity; the non-Catholic Christian or pagan tosses it aside as unworthy of consideration.

This is an outstanding example of the characteristic difference between Catholic Christianity and all other religion; namely, Catholic Christianity exists solely because of the supernatural intimacy between almighty God and His Church. The Catholic who does not know this is a Catholic in name only. The non-Catholic who finds it out very promptly becomes a Catholic because he has been given the Gift of Faith! The fact of infallible protection from error in faith or morals is an item of that supernatural divine intimacy quite as much as is the presence of God Himself in the consecrated Host and the less obvious but equally potent power of God functioning in each of the seven Sacraments.

Not only is God present in the Blessed Sacrament and the Mass, but He is also present in the Teaching Authority of the Church and He is intimately present and intimately interested in every thought and word and act of each one of us. He rejoices in those which are done in union with His love and is wounded and sorrowful over those which offend His love or are indifferent to it. This is not to say that it is impossible for one who is not a Catholic to love and serve God, but I hope that it does help you see the tremendous handicap under which they labor who try to serve God without that certain knowledge of the intimacy of His presence and the intimacy of His present identification with His Church.

His Mystical Body *is* Christ in the world today and that is why it must be the infallible Christ. We know it because He has promised it and because we have seen all of His promises being fulfilled from the very beginning until the present day in spite of all of the obstacles of human frailty. But we should not expect one who has not shared in these promises to be convinced by them alone. We should, however, be better equiped to help the non-Catholic and the non-Christian to clear away the obstacles which have prevented them from accepting this precious truth.

The doctrine of Infallibility provides the believing Catholic with an assurance and confidence which is not to be found in any other pursuit of knowledge, but the observation that it is precious if true is not an argument in favor of its *being* true. In fact, the non-believer would classify it as the number one example of that which is too good to be true. I have said that the book, "Christianity and Infallibility — Both or Neither," helped me greatly in my quest for the true faith. I should, perhaps, have said that it served more as a climax of the quest to make the gift of Faith a perfect treasure, rather than a body of evidence to provide the answer to the quest.

So, while never losing sight of our objective which is to equip ourselves as apostles of Christian reunion, we must remember that we can only enter into Truth by Charity. That is why, with you as well as with the enquirer seeking to learn the Faith, I wish to pave the way for a careful consideration of the evidence for the infallibility of the Teaching Authority of our Church by showing first that the Church is nothing other than the monument of Christ's love embracing every human being born into the world. Just as Christ's love is single and infinite, so the expression of His love offered to you and to me today is single and infinitely individual, as well as infinitely universal.

To start with this knowledge of the nature of the Church, we need only look back to see how it came to be, and who became its members. Why did almighty God come to this insignificant world full of men who had made themselves His enemies? There is just one possible answer — *Love* — infinite, eternal, divine love, brought into the realm of our sense-knowledge by giving infinite power of divine love to the human love of Jesus Christ. "God so loved the world that He gave His only Begotten Son that all who believe in Him should not perish but should possess eternal life." (John 3:16).

Christ's entire life was one continuous demonstration of this love and one continuous search for those who would love Him in return; for those who would become the loving sheep of His Flock for which He, the Good Shepherd, would lay down His life as final supreme act of love. But it is unthinkable that such infinite and binding love would cease to function eternally once the supreme sacrifice of love had ended the earthly life of the God-Man. "If anyone loveth Me, he will keep My word, and My Father shall love him, and We will come to him and make our abode with him. . . And the word that ye hear is not Mine but the Father's Who hath sent Me. (John 14:23-24).

It is baffling, however, to try to support this general notion by choosing from among the many quotations from Scripture. The entire Gospel is saturated with it. In fact, the very word "Gospel" means tidings of joy, tidings of love. God's love is expressed in a thousand ways and proved by as many acts of love. Those who responded with love for Him became the members of His Church. Of these He chose the ones who would project the offer of His love to the men of all time and guaranteed to them that it would be constant for all time and offered in one body of Truth. "All power," He said to them, "is given to Me in heaven and on earth. Going therefore, teach ye all nations; baptizing them in the name of the Father, and of the Son, and of the Holy Spirit; teaching them to observe all things whatsoever *I* have commanded *you*: and behold I am with you all days, even to the consumation of the world." (Matt. 28:18-20).

It is almost impossible for us to see how this last command and promise of Christ can have any other meaning than that God was giving them a guarantee of power with the command to teach *what* He had taught them and what He would hold fast for them by being with them until the consummation of the world. And yet, not long ago a man of good will said to me that he could not see why we should attach such a momentuous meaning to the expression: "behold, I am with you until the consummation of the world." "It might mean," said he, "I am with you in My own way, just as I have always been; or, I am with you just as I am when you say to each other 'Good bye' which means — God be with you."

It would have been a very hollow answer to this young man to say: "Well, we can only enter into Truth by Charity." And yet, that is exactly what the situation proved, because this same young man did enter into that particular truth a few months later, and he did it by the route of Charity.

Taken out of context, the expression "I am with you even to the consummation of the world" could, perhaps, have a meaning less comprehensive than the promise of divine protection of the teaching coupled to the command. But, taken as the final word of God recorded by Saint Matthew, and seen in the light of the love with which the whole of Christ's ministry was committed to these, His first Bishops, love finds it impossible to attach to it a meaning as inconsequential as the one at first suggested by this young man.

These things, however, should not cause us to lose heart for the very reason that *we* know that Christ *is* with His Church until the consummation of the world. It only shows us the utter confidence in Christ with which we must approach the subject. It also shows the union with His will which we must have. For after all, He met with the same misunderstanding because of lack of love in most of those who heard His message from His own lips and of whom He said: "The heart of these people has become gross, and their ears are hard of hearing, and their eyes they have closed, lest perchance they should see with their eyes, and hear with their ears, and understand with their heart, and turn again, and I should heal them." (Matt. 13:15). Christ, indeed, will heal them, but the message must be presented to them, not as the doctrine of men but as the doctrine of *Love*!

CHAPTER XI

FAITH IN ACTION

If the previous chapter has helped to clinch our trust in the FAITH hept current for us by the Holy Spirit acting in the Ordinary Teaching of our Church, it is time to put that Faith into action. This is doubly important in these days when the "Gates of Hell" have demonstrated far too much success in diluting the Faith taught to our children and all too many priests and Religious have demonstrated grave disloyalty and disobedience to the Holy Father.

To most of us who are trying to put our faith into action in these latter days of the twentieth century it is perhaps a little disconcerting to consider the prompting of Christ in this regard. When the Apostles who had been given the power to heal the sick asked Him why they were unable to cure the boy who was tortured by a demon, He said to them: "Indeed, I tell you, if you possess faith like a mustard seed, you may say to this mountain: 'Remove hence to yonder place, and it shall remove; and nothing shall be impossible to you." (Matt. 7:20).

These words of our Lord, however, are not meant to discourage us but to emphasize our need for everlasting TRUST in Him and LOVE for Him who is always ready to reward our trust and our love. This, too, is most important in these present days when science and Atheism have almost succeeded in quenching the fear of hell as a motive for putting faith into action. So let us consider the function of Faith in Action in those Christians who want to be good because they love God and want to be helped to know how best to do His will.

True, the fear of hell should be a compelling motive to goodness, but experience has shown that God allows Satan to invite people to think that it is useless to advertise his home-port because, there being no round-trip tickets, it is better to keep what is out of sight — out of mind as well.

No Catholic and no believer in the authority of the Bible can deny the reality of hell as a state of everlasting punishment for sin. But, human nature being what it is, the love of God is a far more potent incentive to make us try to obey His commandments and to mean it when we say: "Thy will be done." And so, we are going to try to learn to do the will of God by talking about "Faith in Action" for our benefit and for the benefit of those who have not yet found their way to Faith.

Faith alone, is not the goal of our quest. It is the vehicle which takes us to the goal. It is the foundation upon which God builds the mansion of our goal. It is the plant upon which grow the flower and fruit of our goal.

Faith is the necessary beginning of sanctity. But it is only when it functions as a beginning, as a source, as an activator, that it has any merit at all. By itself alone, it is dead, but without it all else is dead.

That is not to say, however, that it is not precious. Christ our Lord, throughout His ministry did little else than plead with His hearers to *believe*. Saint Paul extolled faith to the point where he was misunderstood by some who were careless about his meaning. But Christ and Saint Paul and Saint Peter and Saint John and Saint James, all demanded and extolled faith only *as* a beginning. The faith they demanded contained action within its nature.

The kind of faith that Christ asked for and Saint Paul asked for simply did not exist unless it manifested its nature by works. Saint Paul wrote several chapters to the Romans and the Hebrews about faith *versus* works. But the works he denounced as opposed to faith are the legalistic and artificially distorted perversions of the Mosaic Law, totally devoid of the life-giving faith which made saints among the Jewish Patriarchs of the Old Testament. But the examples of faith that Saint Paul opposes to dead works, are fairly bristling with works that gave them meaning.

It was only malice in some and ignorance in others which could possibly distort the meaning of Saint Paul's writing to claim justification for Martin Luther's maxim: "Sin manfully, but believe more manfully." — or the more modern notion of being "saved" by trust in the mercy of God in spite of corruption of soul. This notion is comparable to that other misleading idea expressed by Martin Luther, that the soul of a man who is "saved" by faith is like a dung-hill covered with snow.

For the same Paul who says: "We argue that a man is justified by faith apart from legal observances" (Rom. 3:28); also says in the same Epistle to the Romans: "Thou art storing up for thyself wrath on the day of wrath and the day of revelation of the just judgment of God who will requite everyone according to his words." (Rom. 2:5-6); and who says to the Corinthians: "And if I possessed utter faith so that I could remove mountains and have not charity, I am nothing." (I. Cor. 13:2).

The same Christ who says: "Whoever believes in Him should not perish, but possess eternal life," (John 3:16) immediately attaches that belief to deeds, for He adds: "He who does according to the Truth comes to the Light so that his deeds may be seen clearly to have been done in God."

So *we* begin to see clearly the meaning of Saint James' words: "I will show thee my faith *by* my works." (James 2:18). The kind of faith Christ gives us in response to our will to believe, cannot exist without manifesting itself in action by conforming to the will of Him who gives us the grace to believe.

To the extent that we fail to measure up to the standard given us by Christ in His sermon on the Mount, which He sums up by saying: "Do you therefore be perfect as your heavenly Father is perfect." (Matt. 5:48) — to that extent we are exhibiting deficiency in our cooperation with what

Saint Paul calls "The measure of faith which God has imparted to each." (Rom. 12-3).

The point that I want to make is this: We should never be insulted if anyone questions the sufficiency of our faith. I include myself very definitely in that admonition. The nearer faith comes to perfection, the nearer do our lives conform to Christ's. The faith of the Blessed Virgin Mary was as perfect as is possible for a human being. And so she was the most perfect member of the human race, excepting only her divine Son. It follows then, that as we must admit deficiency in perfection, so must we strive to increase the efficiency of our faith.

We seek the same goal of sanctity as did the Apostles. Are we less in need of faith then they? It was their petition to Christ to: "Increase our faith," that brought forth from Him the reply: "If you had faith like a grain of mustard seed, you might say to this mulberry tree, 'be thou uprooted and transplanted into the sea,' and it would obey you." (Luke 17:5-6). Indeed, it is recorded many times in the Gospels, that our Lord had to chide His followers for their lack of faith.

Usually the situation was one in which each of us would have displayed the same deficiency. "The boat was beginning to be swamped by the waves; but He was asleep. And they came and awoke Him, crying, 'Lord, save us! We shall be lost! ' And He said to them: "Why are you afraid, you men of little faith? ' " (Matt. 8:24-26).

And again: "But seeing the violence of the waves, Peter became afraid: and, beginning to sink, he cried out, 'Lord, save me! ' Immediately Jesus, extending His hand, seized him and said to him, 'O thou weakling in faith! Why didst thou doubt? ' " (Matt. 14:30-31).

And, as Jesus descended from Mount Tabor a man came to Him saying: "Master, I have brought Thee my son, who is possessed by a dumb spirit ... I asked Thy disciples to expell it but they had not the power." — "Oh you unbelieving generation! " He said in reply. ... "If Thou canst do anything, have pity on us and help us! " "If thou *canst*! " said Jesus to him, "Why, all things are possible to him who be-

lieves." Immediately the father of the child cried aloud and
said: "I do believe! Help Thou my unbelief." (Mark
9:17-25). Each one of us should repeat that ejaculation of
faith and hope not once but many times in every day!

And yet, Saint Peter, guilty of all those deficiencies of
faith, later appears confirmed in faith as steadfast as any
martyr of his time or since. Standing before the very men
who had crucified his Master, he said to them: "Let it be
known to you all ... that by the name of Jesus Christ, the
Nazarene, whom you crucified, whom God raised from the
dead, by Him this man stands in your presence, well ...
there is not another Name under heaven given among men
by which we must be saved." (Acts 4:10).

The deficiencies of faith among the Apostles should not
make us complacent of our own deficiencies: Neither should
the heights of faith to which they were raised make us de-
spair of the hope for the same gift. Should we say: "If faith
is always a free gift from God, it is not our fault if we are
weak? " By no means! God never gives His gifts to the
supine. On the contrary, in His infinite wisdom, He always
gives it in such a way that we can have some part to call our
own by meritorious cooperation with His grace. True, this is
very little, but so is every finite work little compared with
the infinite goodness of God. There is no limit to the faith
He will give us if we dispose ourselves by putting what faith
we have into action!

The Christ of the twentieth century emphasized this when
He said to the mystic Gabrielle Bossis: "Do you want to
practice faith? Do you understand what an elan this would
give to your prayer, your Communion, your every day in-
terior life? Would you like to try? You may be sure that
your hope and love would grow in the same proportion. And
to grow is to come close to Me. (*HE & I* — Editions
Paulines, Vol. II, p. 110).

Now, every Catholic worthy of the name has tremendous
faith to be grateful for, as well as tremendous deficiencies of
faith to be worked at. No one in his right mind could possibly become a Catholic without faith. Of course, the only
motive for practicing religion is the love of God. But love

can be no more secure that the faith it rests on. And that is
why I make so much of faith! We have such a lot of it, and
we have taken so much trouble because of it, that it is
simply a criminal waste of grace if we do not make the most
of it.

*Self-love is the source of every trial and hardship of our
lives*! Yes, I mean just that! Yes, I am even thinking of
those things over which we have no control: sickness, acci-
dents, injury from others, unjust criticism, difficult or un-
pleasant assignments, Not one of them can be a trial except
as it is made so by self-love. And self-love stems from defi-
cient faith every time. The only way to root it out is to cultivate deeper faith. To "stir up the faith that *is* in us."

> **Love of God is Faith in act!**
> **Love of self means Faith is lacked!**

It does not require as much faith as a grain of mustard
seed to see that all these things that look like crosses to self-
love, are really precious gifts, planned by Christ for our welfare. If we can learn to accept them with gratitude, then we
may know that our faith is growing apace. What can we do,
then, to hasten the perfection of our faith? Like a healthy
child, it thrives on exercise. Faith in action is faith on the
mend!

Not only are all our sins, down to the very least, evidence
of weak faith, but every imperfection as well. I just mention
this to show what a very great field we have in which to
work when we wish to exercise and improve our faith by
action.

Is it difficult for you to see that your own annoyance at
a neighbor's imperfection is a signal for you to examine your
own conscience for spots of rust on your faith? A really
finely polished faith in your soul will reflect on your heart
the observation that Christ, to whom even the hairs of your
neighbor's head are all numbered, and Who loves him even as
much as you hope He loves you, has not only the power,
but also the will to deal with his imperfections or downright
faults in the manner best suited to the situation, down to
the least detail, some of which may not be known to you.

This knowledge and will of Christ includes every item in the life and action of every person you know. All those which you have ever noticed, and all the rest which you have ignored. Perhaps this last group includes some of your own imperfections. Perhaps the imperfection that has annoyed you, has been one of your own! This annoyance at one's own faults is unmistakable evidence of self-love: that other name for imperfect faith!

Annoyance or vexation over one's own imperfections and faults is not a virtue, but a vice. The only reaction acceptable to Christ is humble recognition, with a resolve to be conformed to His will. It may surprise you to consider this fine distinction between vexation over faults and humble acceptance of them with a resolve to turn to Christ for a remedy. But this is most important. Vexation is self-love; humble recognition, with calm resolve, is evidence of faith that Christ is really present always and not only aware, but able to provide the remedy.

If the fault is your own, or if you are in charge of a situation and the fault lies within the purview of your responsibility, Christ often permits a subtle but certain index of self-love which even the most fervent self-lover cannot fail to note, if he is willing. It happens when the fault is brought to your attention, either by another or by results. There is just one word that fully describes the true self-lover's reaction. It is a technical word and is, perhaps, a little slangy when used in this sense. But it has a nuance that cannot be supplied by any other word that I know. The word is *alibi*.

Do you ever alibi? If so, and who does not sometimes! — you have work to do on your faith. How can you think that any explanation to relieve you of some of the blame or responsibility has any merit when Christ has been intimately present all the time and knows every detail far better than you do? A man in business puts his trust in the associate who never offers an alibi. How much more is this quality an evidence of integrity and good faith in our dealings with Christ in all our activities in the world, as well as in our spiritual affairs!

Another sure sign of defect in faith is a stubborn reluctance to accept the spiritual guidance provided by Christ in our Pastor, our Confessor or our spiritual adviser. I do not mean that situations never arise where matters of conscience need consultation for settlement. Holy Mother Church well recognizes this and makes provision for the safety of conscience of every soul. What I do mean is this: It is an obvious fact that pastors and confessors and spiritual advisers differ in experience and in method of teaching, some perhaps with grave fault. It is equally obvious that no two people see precisely eye-to-eye debatable problems of moral theology. When a person finds himself "shopping around" to find a confessor or an adviser who will give an answer such as he has preconceived he wants the answer to be, he is dangerously near to action that says to Christ: "I do not trust your handling of my affairs."

The same is true of any person who too frequently resorts to criticism of his associates or his superiors, spiritual or temporal. Even though these may too frequently be wrong, and in these days some priests seem to be inspired by malice to *be* wrong, nevertheless, the docile soul, the one who is trying to be receptive of a deep supernatural faith, is content to leave these matters to the capable management of Christ whom he trusts and believes in the works of His hands.

Now, I beg you not to think how appropriately these words apply to someone else. They are addressed to each reader as well as to the writer himself, personally and individually. They apply to me and I believe they apply to every one I have ever known, at least sometimes – and I have known some very holy souls. They apply equally to those inclined to scruples, as to those whose consciences are perhaps a little less than tender. There never will be one of us who is entirely free from the need of examining his defects of faith. The soul most in need of this warning is often not as ready to accept it as is one with deeper faith.

There are so many, many ways our wretched self-love has of insinuating itself into our poor little "mustard seed" of faith that we simply must admit the need of help, and learn to know all the forms it takes. Humility and obedience are, of course, the sworn enemies of self-love and so are impossible without deep faith.

Other manifestations of self-love are: curiosity, love of novelty, desire to be thought progressive in matters of faith and morals. The terrifying truth is that when these tendencies are not checked by a submissive active discipline of the will, God allows grace to be withdrawn and basic faith to wane so that even a scholarly priest may lose his faith and become that most pitiful of all human beings, an apostate.

And so we see that we carry this tremendously important, this essential gift of supernatural faith in earthen vessels. The fragility of our faith because of the wounds in our human nature; our utter dependence upon God to receive it and to keep it; all these make it clear why Saint Paul, that most fervent lover of men's souls, warns us: "Let him who thinketh he standeth take heed lest he fall." (I. Cor. 10:12) — why he wrote to the Phillipians saying: "My dearly beloved . . . work out your salvation with fear and trembling, for it is God who is effecting in you the power both to will and to act for the fulfillment of His good pleasure." (Phil. 2:12-13).

But Saint Paul was never one to leave us in danger of scruples or on the verge of dispair. He urges us by these sentiments to cherish our faith and to work at it, to pray for it and to realize that by our docility and our willing union with the will of God, we have an infallible security that God will not deprive us of it.

Having done this, Saint Paul continues: "Act always without murmurs and discussions, so that you may become faultless and sincere, blameless children of God in the midst of a crooked and perverse generation, among whom you appear as luminaries in the world. (Phil. 2:14-16).

So, let us never forget that this gift of God can be strengthened and made more secure and effective by our cooperation in union with His will. Whenever any unpleasantness arises, either from persons or things or within ourselves, let us immediately check it by a calm, untroubled act of faith, leaving all things in the safe hands of Christ in whom we live and move and have our being.

CHAPTER XII

MARY: MOTHER OF DIVINE GRACE

The very first thing needed to put faith into effective action is abundant grace from the throne of God. It is the supernatural guidance of grace that permits each one of us to do our part in the unfolding of God's perfect plan for calling *Menders* to His service.

It is important, therefore, that we should be reminded of the precious privilege which God has given us by making His Mother to be our Mother and our Mediatrix of Divine Grace. This is especially important in view of the objective of our quest which is primarily a campaign of prayer to beseech God to rout the evil in the Church that seems to be opening wide the Gates of Hell for a final devastating attack upon our stronghold.

It has been made clear to us many times that it is God's strategy to use the weak to overcome those who are apparently strong in the eyes of the world. And so it is to be expected that the campaign of *mending* to which God is inviting all of us, should be a uniting in prayer made strong by the intercession of the Mother of Divine Grace whom He has given us.

Her appeal is still the same; ready and waiting to obtain for us the grace to win the goal of Fatima by organizing into groups and also to work singly to make the Rosary God's weapon of Victory. All the Rosaries since Fatima are in

God's Armory. He asks us now to make up for what has been left undone in the past. Let us turn, then, to reassure ourselves of the Source of grace and the help God wishes us to receive from Mary, our Mother and Mediatrix of all grace.

This has been beautifully expressed in the following words taken from one of the twelve Encyclical Letters written by Pope Leo XIII extolling the Blessed Virgin Mary.

> **"How unerringly right are Christian souls when they turn to Mary for help as though impelled by an instinct of nature, confidently sharing with her their future hopes and past achievements, their sorrows and joys, commending themselves like children to the care of a bountiful Mother."** (Adjutricem Populi — Leo XIII — 9-5-1895 P.D. p. 103).

So it is under the title of this Chapter, Mary: Mother of Divine Grace, that I wish to urge each one of you to appreciate with me, in the fullness of its reality, the privilege which we enjoy because Mary *is* our Mother of Divine Grace. I say this because it is in the world of grace that all of the fruits of our faith are given to us.

It is regrettable, however, that it cannot be said that we Catholics fully appreciate that important fact. And so it is to solicit the help of Our Lady, Mother of Divine Grace, to draw many millions into the campaign of prayer of the Army of *Menders*, that I wish to explore this idea with you.

To be honest with you, my enthusiasm for this idea all stems from a simple question which was asked of me by a young lady who came to me for guidance. She had come home from Mass on the previous Sunday somewhat disturbed by the statement made by the priest in his sermon that man can reach God "only through Mary." "How," she wished to know, "can that be reconciled with the recitation of the 'Our Father' and how can it be true as we receive Our Lord in Holy Communion?" "Furthermore," she said, "what is the use of praying to Saint Joseph or any of the saints if they have to take it to Our Lady and then she takes it to God?" I tried to answer her question by explaining the common teaching of the Church that Christ has made it known to us that He has chosen from all eternity that His

Mother should be the Mediatrix of all graces coming from Him to the children of men.

The more I thought about my answer afterward, however, the more I realized that I had never really explored the full meaning of that precious doctrine myself, nor had I fully appreciated how intimately it blesses Catholics in particular. I discussed it at length with my monastic confreres and since then have made a breathless excursion into the immense treasury of doctrinal and spiritual literature which gives a wealth of guidance and inspiration along these lines.

My first reaction is one of gratitude for my Faith. Next I am surprised that in my long-standing sense of devotion to and confidence in Our Lady, I am only beginning to see the true meaning of her status as Mediatrix of Graces. This gives me a keen desire to explore it further and to invite you to share it with me.

At the outset I think it will be helpful for me to explain why I have paid so little attention in the past to the study of the doctrine of Our Lady as Mediatrix of all Graces. In fact, I should perhaps admit that I have shied away from it because it has seemed unnatural to me. The sole reason for passing it by has been that the notion of mediatrix has had a connotation of placing between me and the Source of all good a human authority which, however loving it might be, was hard to reconcile with the notion of the indwelling presence of the divinity within my own soul and the very special presence of Christ in the Blessed Sacrament at Mass and in the grace of other Sacraments. Even the notion of a willing channel through which my petitions must pass to God and the fruits of His love come to me seemed like a separation from the warmth of my access to God-The-Son.

This notion was heightened rather than lessened for me by the attempt to explain the relationship by likening the Blessed Virgin to the "Neck" of the Mystical Body of Christ which unites rather than separates all the members and gives them union with the life-giving source of power and grace in Christ the Head. To me this is a particularly unfortunate simile as being, in itself, so sterile of the attributes of the Blessed Virgin our Mother.

The only hope of making it attractive is to remember that the titles of her Litany: "Tower of David" and "Tower of Ivory", stems from appropriation to her of the references to the Bride in the Old Testament Canticle of Canticles: "Thy neck rising proudly, nobly adorned, like David's embattled tower" from Chapter Four, verse four, and, "Thy neck rising proudly like a tower, but all of ivory" from Chapter Seven, verse four. But it is still difficult for me to find help in using the simile to illustrate the joyous love which I feel toward my Mother of Divine Grace.

To speak of her as the *heart* of the Mystical Body is more attractive because we are all used to thinking of the heart as the seat of love in our human relations. But it is really still less appropriate when used as a simile in reference to Mary as the Mediatrix of all Graces.

I must, however, immediately qualify my own choice in the matter by admitting that both of these comparisons are found to be helpful by a great many people and are to be found in the writings of some of our great saints, notably Saint Bernard.

It is possible, too, that our understanding of her role is confused by the use of that word "Mediatrix." That title is often used and is legitimate if it is properly understood although no one denies that Christ is the sole Mediator between God and man since He alone *is* God and Man.

It is as Queen-Mother that she is Mediatrix. Her rule is a rule of love united with *His* rule of love and power.

For myself, I have found another comparison which completely satisfies me and redoubles my desire to be brought into union with Christ entirely in the arms of my Mother in the manner made so beautifully obvious by Cardinal Suenens in his very satisfying book entitled: *MARY THE MOTHER OF GOD*.

The reference to Mary as our Mother is, of course, as old as Christianity itself since it was first used by Christ on the Cross. I shall not say that He "instituted" its use, but rather that He made it known as a fact of God's election. The contribution made by Cardinal Suenens toward confidence in the doctrine of Mary's status as Mediatrix of all Graces lies in the simple clarity with which he has shown us exactly how it is to be understood.

The obscurity which needs to be cleared away may stem from our failure to distinguish clearly the difference between the two worlds in which we live; the world of nature, and the world of supernature which is the world of grace. God is the Author and Owner and Omnipotent Preserver of both, but His relationship to the body and soul of each one of us in each is very literally "worlds apart".

We have this universe with all its countless suns and satellites and this earth with all its equipment to nourish the bodies and souls of men. All is God's handiwork, all is completely under His control. All has been drawn by Him out of nothing. None of it would continue to exist from moment to moment were it not for the intimate presence and power of God. Everything behaves according to the nature which God has planned for it, plays its part in the wonderfully ordered world of nature.

God might have chosen to leave it at that and man might never have been the wiser. There would be mothers and sons and daughters succeeding one another and passing on into an immortal state of natural existence with only a distant knowledge of God. But, thanks be to God, He did not choose to leave it at that. It was not for that that He created men, but for a world of glory, a world of grace, a supernatural world, in which He would be united with us in an eternal union of happiness and love which springs from knowing Him as He is.

The natural world is perceived by our five natural senses. The full perception of the supernatural world will require faculties which we do not now possess. That does not mean, however, that it is any less real than this world in which we live where God has placed us to train us to be His dearest children in the world of glory. Neither does it mean that we have no access to the supernatural world here and now. Our access, however, is at a gateway which inexorably separates the two worlds — the gateway of supernatural faith.

This gate is opened by the gift of God and no part of the supernatural world is found on the outer side of the gate except the invitation to knock which we call "actual grace". Once the gate is opened to us and entrance to the supernatural world is gained, we are made members of it, in accordance with the command of Christ, by the Sacrament of Baptism and the indwelling presence of the Holy Spirit. "Unless one is born of water and the Spirit, one cannot enter the Kingdom of God." (John 3:5).

The Catholic Church is staged in the natural world but all of its most important action is in the supernatural world known here only by faith. The Church, as Christ promised, is visible to our senses in its equipment and in its members and above all in the form of its worship. Its Sacrifice and Sacraments and official prayer life are all carried on in accordance with Christ's command.

But, saturating and superseding all that can be seen with the eye, is the divine life-giving Spirit, "for whom" as Christ said, "the world can find no room, because it cannot see Him, cannot recognize Him. But you are to recognize Him; He will be at your side forever — He will teach you all things and will remind you of all that I have told you ... He shall guide you into all truth." (John 14:17 & 16:13).

It is this which makes the Church the infallible and imperishable means of salvation for all men born into this world. It unites the Church with the wholly supernatural world united with God in the Beatific Vision whence comes all grace, all power, and to whom all prayer and worship is directed.

It is there that Christ sits at the right hand of God the Father. He is the source of our Redemption, the sole Mediator of the fruits of our salvation. There also sits at His right hand the one perfect member of the human race whom He has chosen and made His Queen-Mother. Who, by His election is also Queen above all angels and saints and sinners.

Christ represented us when He made her His natural mother and thereby gave her the precious heritage of being the supernatural Mother of all whom the Father would draw to Him. This He confirmed on the Cross in the person of Saint John and has taught ever since by His infallible Church.

She stands united with Christ in God. We stand united
with her in Christ. All prayer, all worship is offered to God
by the human family in union with our Mother of Grace. All
the fruits of our prayer and worship come from the source
which is Christ, as if we all sat at a banquet table where our
Queen-Mother presides in union with Christ and in union
with us dispenses them to us — not as a channel — but by
the supernatural tie of Maternity.

And here Cardinal Suenens furnishes the most enlighten-
ing concept of all, to help us to appreciate Our Lady's role.
While she is called, and is, our Mother, her relationship to us
is totally in the supernatural world of grace. It is probably
physical and is certainly real. It is divided from her natural
maternity of Christ as well as her moral or physical participation with Him in His Passion.

Its identification with maternity is, however, clinched by
two essential characteristics, mother love, and child dependence. Mary presides over her children with a love that is all
but infinite and welcomes and encourages their approach to
God through prayer and the Sacraments and the Sacrifice of
Mass, and by the will of God she dispenses to them the
fruits of their intentions in both the natural and supernatural
worlds.

Mary does not dwell within the soul of her children. That
is the property of the Spirit of God which enlivens the soul
and makes it capable of union with Him. It is this union,
however, that is strengthened by the gifts which are dis-
pensed by Mary. Our dependance upon Mary is proportion-
ate to our union with her in Christ. And so, as we grow in
grace, we reverse the process of natural maturity and, as
Christ willed it, we become as little children being nourished
by our Mother. It then becomes more and more natural to
us to look to her for everything we need.

And so this is the economy of salvation! On earth, Christ
has provided us with His One, Holy, Catholic and Apostolic
Church to bring salvation to all men for whom He shed His
Blood. In heaven He sits enthroned in His majesty and has

placed at His right hand her whom He had chosen from all eternity to be the means of His Incarnation and to share with Him His redeeming Passion.

He is the Mediator and source of all grace to men. She is the Mediatrix chosen by Him as the Mother of Divine Grace. By her loving intercession He sends His Spirit to dwell in the souls of those who love Him and keep His commandments. How do we know all this? There is only one answer: because God told us so and His Church has taught us this from the very beginning.

And so all men must find salvation through His Church on earth. Those who, without their own fault, do not know this, but wish with all their hearts to do God's will and keep His commandments, may share in this salvation, but always, even unknowingly, through His Church. Those who learn to know this truth and refuse to use the means God has provided, thereby expel God from their souls and, if they do not repent, put themselves beyond the reach of salvation.

Those who seek God and love Him with true devotion and with contrition for their sins are especially loved by His· Mother. She intercedes for them and obtains grace for them even though they do not know that she is their Mother of Divine Grace. Those who know this and refuse the love she offers them, have no access to Christ. In the words of Pope Saint Pius X: "Miserable and unhappy are they who neglect her on the pretense that they thus honor Christ. They forget that 'the Child is not found without Mary His Mother.'" The oil is gone from their lamp and charity is extinguished. (Ad Diem Illum – P.D. p. 141)

But happy those who, ever more closely united with her in love, become as her littlest children and, as my little three-year-old niece used to say to her mother after the Red Cross meetings of World-War-Two: "To these do we cry, poor *bandaged* children of Eve." And then, at last, her children, as if yet unborn, offer her perfect love as their intercessor with God — and receive from Him the everlasting love which He bestows upon His Chosen Queen of Heaven.

In the words of the Book of Wisdom: "She is an incorruptible treasure to men, which they that use become the friends of God.

I promise you that the rest of my life will be aimed at reaching God — only through Mary, my Mother!

CHAPTER XIII

THE MEANING OF THE FEAR
OF GOD FOR MENDERS

If we are now joyfully seated at the banquet table loaded by our Savior with all the graces needed for valiant MENDERS, and presided over by His Queen-Mother, there is an item of our relationship to our divine Provider which needs to be clarified. It is contained in the following words from the opening chapter of the Book of Ecclesiasticus:

> **"The fear of the Lord is wisdom's crown: with this, peace and health are thine to enjoy: this fear itself is God's gift, no less than the wisdom which is counted out under His eyes." (Ecclus. 1:22-23 Knox).**

There are several kinds of fear which stem from the impact of the awful majesty of God upon the understanding of His creatures. I say, "several kinds", because there is a very great difference of species as well as of degree.

The underlying principles of these various kinds of fear of God run a wide gamut — all the way from remote separation from God and deadly hatred of His majesty — up to the last-but-one step before the perfect charity that casteth out fear, spoken of by Saint John in his first Epistle (4:18), which is quoted by Saint Benedict in his Holy Rule for Monks. Moreover, the perfect Charity possessed by the Son of God in His Incarnation includes, as we are told by the

Prophet Isaias (11:1-3), together with the other Gifts of the Spirit of God which rest upon Him: "and ever the fear of the Lord shall fill His heart."

I mention this at the outset to show you that, while the virtuous fear of God is not precisely like Charity, which knows no limit either of intensity or duration, still, as a virtue, it accompanies and perfects Charity right up to and including the Beatific Vision. It is to be cultivated and cherished and prayed for during all of our sojourn in this vale of tears. It is because the evil connotation of some kinds of fear of God lessen our appreciation of it as a virtue, that I wish to try to separate the two in your mind for all the future!

So — with that in mind, let us look at some of the kinds and degrees of fear that spring from knowledge of God's infinite majesty. First, and perhaps most common among men, we have the fear of God-the-Unknown. We believe that human reason teaches us of the existence of God, albeit very imperfectly. This being true, it follows that even the untutored savage and the child just coming into the possession of reason, have *some* concept of the existence of the Creator and Governor of the universe, but their acknowledgement of this concept is expressed in fear of the unknown — this very indefinitely — personal Power. This fear, moreover, stems from self-love and gives rise to a response of propitiation expressed, perhaps, in prayer and sacrifices. It is especially intense in the presence of the great manifestations of the power of nature such as the tornado, the thunder storm, the earthquake.

Next, we have a far different kind of fear of God found in the Devil and his angels. This, too, stems from self-love, but there the likeness ends! Far from being unknown, the majesty of God's justice is all too well known and is feared with a hatred generated by consummate pride.

The fear of God which resides in the souls of the reprobate in hell is similar to the fear which is impressed upon the devils, but it differs in proportion to the difference between human nature and angelic nature.

Another fear of God in hateful form is found among the men who surround us in this world. This fear is not yet confirmed in hate although it, too, stems from self-love and pride. This is the fear which resides in the souls of our fellow way-farers who are living in a state of mortal sin. It expresses itself in a great variety of acts, from open persecution of the Church, which seeks to give the lie to the cause of the fear by extinguishing it from the face of the earth, to the cowardly fear which seeks to extinguish conscience by plumbing further into the depths of mortal sin. This is the kind of fear of God which furnished the motive for the crucifixion of Christ.

Then comes that tremendous group living in the world of today whose fear is hard to classify: those who consider themselves Christians but still remain aloof from the practice of Faith. The case of each one of these is unique and is different from the rest. No one can know for certain the actual state of their souls. But the fear of most of them is much like the fear of God-the-unknown only in a more sophisticated form. It expresses itself in the more sophisticated acts of philanthropy and humanism.

And finally, among those who fear God for motives of self-love, we have those who manage to *keep* out or *get* out of the meshes of mortal sin, but who do not really hate sin and would turn back to sin were it not for the fear of hell. This is servile or slavish fear.

All of these souls except those already damned should be the objects of our most fervent prayers. They need prayers more than all the rest of mankind. Many of the saints and holy priests and people spend much of their time praying for the souls in Purgatory. Indeed, we know from revelation that this is a very pious work of charity. For myself, however, and with the motive of the fear of God's justice, I prefer to do my utmost in prayer to beg to have a part as Christ's instrument in obtaining His grace of redemption for the lost sheep who, but for that grace, would go to hell. The difference between Purgatory and Heaven is indeed great, but the difference between Purgatory and hell is infinte!

With this motive in mind, then, let us turn our thoughts to the true holy fear of God which is one of the seven precious gifts of the Holy Spirit and which is a most necessary part of the equipment needed for the Army of *Menders* which we are hoping to promote. The motive of reverential or filial fear which accompanies the indwelling of the Holy Spirit and which, we are told, reposed even in the heart of the Incarnate Word Himself, is just the opposite of the motive of servile fear or the fear of hate.

The Gift of Fear is really an expression of love of the highest order. It is true charity which is love of benevolence toward God. It cannot consent — in oneself or in the rest of creation — to a failure to do one's best for God's glory. It is truly fear, but its action is to make us anxious lest our weakness, or the weakness of others, will make us less than as good as God wants us to be, and so disappointing to Him who has been so bountiful in His goodness to us.

The Gift of Fear not only stirs us to pray for those who seem to be in the greatest danger of offending the goodness of God and so of losing the only real good that this life has to offer, but it makes us always aware that it is only the goodness of God that helps us to keep ourselves out of that same state. Thus it helps us to realize that it is only by constant vigilance and cooperation with grace that we have any assurance that we will be able to end our lives, persevering in a state of grace.

This fear and trembling lest we offend God is the best antidote for the poison of self-love, but it is not at all a despairing fear. On the contrary, it is coupled with confidence in God which stimulates that precious virtue of hope together with distrust of self which breeds humility and temperance, without which real sanctity is almost impossible.

With this perspective, we are able to grasp the true meaning of the definition of the Gift of Fear which is given by the great theologian of the spiritual life, Adolphe Tanquerey: "A gift which inclines our will to a filial respect for God, removes us from sin displeasing to Him, and gives us hope in the power of His help."

We are now ready to study the means of cultivating this most efficacious Gift of Fear by looking at the various degrees of its possession in the upward scale stemming from love of God and distrust of self, just as we looked at the degrees downward of the wrong kind of fear stemming from self-love and hatred of God. It must be remembered, of course, that all these gifts of the Holy Spirit are made available to us at Baptism, but in order to avail ourselves of their fruits, they must be nourished and cultivated.

The first or lowest degree of cultivation of the Gift of Fear includes all those who have learned to hate sin because it offends God, but whose will is weak and insecure against the sins of frailty. These may fall often, but their horror of offending the good God causes them to hasten to His rescuing arms whenever temptation assails.

The saints all rise above this degree, but the very working of the Gift of Fear itself keeps them thinking all their lives that they have not succeeded in rising above it. It follows that we who are seeking to *mend* the evil in the world for God's sake, are very much involved. The example of Saint Vincent de Paul's fear that he would find himself deprived of faith, which I have quoted elsewhere, should convince us that there is not one of us who is exempt from the wisdom of this notion. At least, the saints all realize that it is only God's continued goodness that keeps them from dropping back into the first degree after they have emerged from it.

The second degree of cultivation of the Gift of Fear is found in those whose wills are strengthened by the vivid and fervent contrition and repentance which is generated by the Gift itself. Thus the reverential fear and love of God keeps these souls free from all deliberate sin.

The third degree in the upward urge of the Gift of Fear is acquired by those souls whose sense of weakness and contrition begins to generate true humility in their hearts. Indeed, Saint Benedict, in his Holy Rule for Monks, specifies the fear of God as the source of the first degree of humility. Saint Benedict's description of the first degree of humility in Chapter Seven of his Holy Rule gives a wonderful example of the working of the Gift of Fear. Here is the way he expresses it:

"The first degree of humility, then, is that a man always keep the fear of God before his eyes, avoiding all forgetfulness; and that he be ever mindful of all that God hath commanded, bethinking himself that those who despise God will be consumed in hell for their sins, and that life everlasting is prepared for them that fear Him. And keeping himself at all times from sin and vice, whether of the thoughts, the tongue, the hands, the feet, or his own will, let him thus hasten to cut off the desires of the flesh."

That all the degrees of humility stem from the Gift of Fear is shown by Saint Benedict in the summation found in his description of the twelfth degree of humility where he says: "Let him ever think of the guilt of his sins and imagine himself already present before the terrible judgment seat of God: always saying in his heart what the Publican in the Gospel said with eyes cast down, 'O God be merciful to me a sinner.'"

The fourth upward movement of the Gift of Fear comes as love begins to supersede and hope gains strength, bringing with it peace of soul and increased confidence in God. Confidence in God is a very logical concomitant of a high degree of reverential fear.

Humility and Hope, these two fruits of the Gift of Fear, combine to produce perfect reverence which constitutes the fifth degree and makes us always in awe before God's sovereign majesty, always mindful that even the slightest sin constitutes an offense against His Goodness.

This cannot help but fill our hearts with humble contrition — that true reverential fear — which the Heart of God cannot resist. He then begins to bestow upon us that perfect Charity which constitutes the sixth and highest perfection of the Gift of Fear which, while it casts out fear in one sense, still keeps it as a balance wheel to remind us of our weakness as long as we remain in this vale of tears.

Saint John, in his first Epistle, explains this state beautifully as what might be called a contest between fear and love as one reaches a true appreciation of both. . .

"God is love," he says, "he who dwells in love dwells in God, and God in him. That our life in the world should be like His, means that His love has had its way with us to the full, so that we can meet the day of judgment with confidence. Love has no room for fear; and indeed, love drives out fear when it is perfect love, since fear only serves for correction. The man who is still afraid has not yet reached the full measure of love." (I. John 4:17-18).

So, fear is not to be despised but should serve as correction to keep each one of us always alert to God's invitation to put utter confidence in His love for us. This love makes His power and wisdom available to us and invites our love to quiet even the depths of reverential fear.

Let me emphasize that these degrees of efficacy of the Gift of Fear are not necessarily acquired one-by-one. Indeed, all six degrees of this Gift interact with its fruits — humility, contrition, temperance, hope — to generate and increase, each the others.

I think, perhaps, the best use we can make of this Gift of Fear is to allow it to make more effective our examination of conscience, not only before confession, but every day and always. We, who are making, or planning to make, our profession the quest of the Army of *Menders*, should have reached a stage where we are at least partly successful in avoiding deliberate sin, even deliberate venial sin. So, instead of feeling hypocritical over finding matter for confession, let us rather emphasize contrition for our weakness and the smaller faults which swarm into our daily lives no matter how faithfully we may try to master them. Let us frequently think of the words of the "Miserere": "A contrite and humbled heart O God, thou wilt not despise." The more we share in Christ's hatred of sin and in His humility, the greater will be our pardon. Especially should we examine our consciences lest we become casual toward God in the Blessed Sacrament and be unmindful of the majesty of His Presence which He humiliates Himself to bring so close to us.

Saint Catherine of Sienna expresses her love of God in terms of reverential fear expelling from her heart and will all that is not God's will. I wish to end this chapter with her sentiments in your thoughts and hope that you will wish to make them your own: "Whether I eat or whether I drink, whether I speak or keep silent, whether I am asleep or whether awake, whether I see or hear or think; whether I am in the Church or in the house or in the market place; whether I am sick or well, whether I live or die, in each hour and at every moment of my life, whether it is for myself or for my neighbor, I will that all be in God and for God! ... If I knew of anything in me or coming from me — any thought, any word, any work, any movement, small as it may be, which is not for the glory of God — I would certainly tear it out of my life, it horrifies me; I disavow it and refuse to acknowledge it as mine."

CHAPTER XIV

CHRIST'S PRESENCE CLINCHES FAITH

In these days of turmoil in the Church and in the world one can easily be tempted to cry out to Jesus Christ to give just a tiny glimpse of His presence that will fortify his faith against the many occasions for doubt. Such thoughts are indeed natural but the supernatural answer is that this easy way that you seek is precisely not what you are here for! Constant everlasting *trust* in God's presence is the discipline that will find the answer in God's love and God's grace.

Christ made this clear to His immediate disciples when He was preparing them for the work which He had planned for them to carry God's Revelation down the corridor of time until the end of the world. Near the end of His discourse, as reported by Saint Luke, He illustrated His wish for them by telling the parable of "the unjust judge" with these words:

> "This widow wearies me: I will give her redress, or she will wear Me down at last with her visits." "Listen," the Lord said, "to the words of the unjust judge, and tell Me, will not God give redress to His elect, when they are crying out to Him day and night? Will He not be impatient with their wrongs? I tell you He will give them redress with all speed. But ah, when the Son of Man comes, will He find faith left on the earth?" (Luke 18:5-8).

In His discourse our Lord had warned His hearers of the difficulties which they and their successors would experience as a result of the hardness of heart and resistance to grace of those to whom He was sending them. He warned particularly, as we can so easily see now, of the growing of difficulties as time advances and the end of the world draws nearer. He showed them how the attraction of the material world would deceive many and the pride of intellect would lead men to put their faith in the findings of science as if it were independent of God the maker of all things.

He showed them how God allows such false prophets as this faithless judge to prove those who will persevere in their trust in God — *come what may!* He showed them that God's purpose in creating this world and this universe is to prove those who will not be led astray and will not follow those who falsely cry: "Look, He is here! Look, He is there!"

He then warned them that as times grow more perilous, they must fortify their faith and keep it nourished by constant trusting prayer. He compared the plight of the poor widow with that of each of us in every age who has need to persevere in the prayer of faith. The widow finally obtained redress for the wrongs done to her by the intensity of her prayer which simply wore out the resistance of the unjust judge. On the other hand, our prayer of faith is addressed to a loving God who only allows evil in order to show His dear ones the utter necessity of His help. He answers this prayer of faith by securing our trust in the means of salvation and the plan of salvation which He has provided.

But, the climax of Christ's warning applies especially to us in this post-conciliar twentieth century. Turmoil and doubt and disobedience and neglect of the plan of salvation so dearly won for us by Christ, surround us on every side. Christ gives a compelling incentive for the prayer of faith when He asks: "When the Son of Man comes, will He find faith upon the earth?" This question reminds us of the possible sequel to the situation already present in the world which Christ foretold with these words:

> **"And many shall fall away... And many false prophets will arise and mislead many. And on account of the increasing**

lawlessness, the love of the majority will be chilled. But he who perseveres to the end, he it is who shall be saved." (Matt. 24:10-13).

Christ brought to completion the entire body of revelation which God deemed fit to prove and fortify those whom He wished to choose for His companions in the eternal joy of heaven. He not only brought to completion this body of revelation, but He caused it to contain specific details as to how it would be managed to accomplish its purpose for the benefit of all future generations. This He did by establishing a Teaching College with a command and a promise of divine authority and divine assistance and divine equipment and divine aids which we know as the Sacraments of Grace.

The summation of His often repeated commands and His many promises of divine backing is contained in the last two verses of Saint Matthew's Gospel which I have quoted more than once:

"All authority is given to Me in heaven and on earth. Go, therefore, and make disciples of all nations, baptizing them in the Name of the Father and of the Son and of the Holy Spirit; teaching them to observe all whatever I have commanded you: and lo, I am with you throughout all time, even until the consummation of the world!" (Matt. 28:18-20).

These words were addressed to the eleven Apostles by the Risen-Christ shortly before He took His leave of them to return to His eternal Kingdom from which He would guide them by the abiding and indwelling presence of His Holy Spirit. This is, indeed, an appropriate unfolding of God's plan for revealing to us, here in North America today this Deposit of Faith which Christ had placed in the custody of His first Bishops. He had commanded them to launch the final harvest of souls by means of the Church, the Sacraments, and the Teaching Body which He would always guide.

After giving this instruction, Christ told His chosen ones to remain in seclusion in the Cenacle in Jerusalem until they were "invested with power from on high" (Luke 14:49). It was really a prodigious apostolate upon which they were to be sent. So a retreat of ten days was most appropriate to transform their shattered frailty, demonstrated by their behavior during the time of Christ's Passion, into an utterly unconditional commitment of trust and confidence when God the Holy Spirit entered into their souls at Pentecost. The fortification brought about by this retreat prepared all of those present for its climax — the first uniting of the natural and the supernatural into the true and concrete manifestation of the Church which Christ had promised.

This assembly, then, constituted the whole of the Mystical Body of Christ. That is, it was the human matrix planned by Christ and divinely empowered by the Holy Spirit to proceed to the end of time. It furnished the continued manifestation of Christ's physical body now glorified and permeating all that represented it on earth.

There was the Mother of God, now appointed by Christ as the Mother of Men, and personifying the Church as the creature-link with the uncreated divine Person of her Son. There was the Teaching Church, Saint Peter, the Vicar of the Divine Head, and his eleven Bishops, one newly elected, now ready to function in accordance with Christ's command. There was the Church-Believing, one hundred-odd intimate witnesses who had taken refuge with the Apostles and now were fortified by the certain indwelling of the Holy Spirit. These believers were now ready to exhibit their fortitude in such a way as to drive Saint Peter's words into the hearts of three thousand new faithful supporters on the same day and many more during the succeeding days of constancy in the face of immediate persecution.

Thus we have a description of the infant Church fully equipped and launched on its perennial mission in accordance with Christ's command to: "Go into the whole world and proclaim the Gospel to all creation . . . and they went forth and preached everywhere, the Lord working with them and confirming the Word by the signs that followed. (Mark 16:15 & 20). And this they have been doing in full vigor and increasing vitality from the middle of the fourth decade of the first century to the present eighth decade of the twentieth century.

The fact that the description of its beginning was put into writing in a variety of accounts by those who were its witnesses or their immediate disciples, has no bearing whatever on the nature of its function. The Church was put into motion by Christ. It has always been and always will be His complete and perfect society of salvation. It consists of a teaching body instituted and empowered and perpetuated by Christ, and a believing-body which has received the entire Deposit of Faith given it by Christ and divinely guarded by the Holy Spirit.

Quite likely there was some writing connected with this teaching from the very beginning, just as preachers make their notes and manuscripts today. But the project put in motion by Christ was a preaching project to carry His word to men at a time when, for centuries to come, means of communication other than preaching were almost non-existent compared with today. Obviously, it would have been very short-lived were it not for the fact that the Holy Spirit of Truth actually did — "guide them into all truth" (John 16:13), and the Lord actually did — "confirm the Word by the signs that followed." (Mark 16:20).

What I want to ask you to consider carefully in this connection is the length of time that the Catholic Church functioned and the amazing expansion which it achieved against the most determined persecution the world has ever seen, without recourse to what we now call the New Testament. It is certainly safe to say that for the first twenty years the New Testament was non-existent. For the first century only fragments of it were in the hands of the preachers themselves as it was being written by them and used by them to aid them in their preaching.

And one more thought: for twenty years the New Testament was non-existent. Twenty years seems like nearly nothing compared with twenty centuries, but what about twenty years of your own life, say from age six to age twenty-six? For most people that twenty years constitutes the entire educational lifetime; it determines their capital-fund of culture and of religion. In other words, for a whole educational lifetime all of Revelation except its roots contained in the Old Testament was brought to the minds of an ever-increasing throng in the Church-Believing by preaching alone. And almost the same condition continued for the next four centuries until the Church was firmly established as the Christian Church of the Roman Empire.

It was inevitable, of course, that the preachers notes should be gradually expanded into Gospels and Epistles. Indeed, it was obviously God's will that they should be, but they all came into existence as an aid to the execution of the command of Christ to *preach* the Gospel to every creature and they have been used as such ever since.

At this point it is important for you to understand that I am not in any slightest way belittling the importance or the relevance or the utter necessity of the New Testament. It is the inspired Word of God literally authored by Him "for us men and for our salvation." It contains all of that part of the Revelation given by Christ to the Apostles which God intended that we should have in writing. It expresses that Revelation in exactly the terms which God caused to be chosen for its expression. That is, God chose exactly the men of their time, to use exactly the language of their milieu, and inspired them to report exactly what they did report.

And here is my thesis: God has caused the entire Bible to be presented to us exactly as it is today to make it obvious to those who are willing to believe, that Project Sainthood is to be attained by each individual traveler in this Vale of Tears in the manner which came from the lips of God; namely, by hearing and believing and behaving in accordance with that belief. And let me repeat that this does not detract in any way from the importance of the Bible and Bible-reading in our lives.

As a matter of fact, "hearing" in our day necessarily includes the words spoken by those who have gone before us. Hearing must include words of those very ones to whom God said: "He who hears you hears Me; and he who rejects you rejects Me; and he who rejects Me rejects Him who sent Me. (Luke 10:16).

God's message to you and me is brought to us by men whom He has chosen all down the centuries from Peter and the Apostles to Paul VI and the Bishops of the Second Vatican Council. God intends that we should look to them for guidance because of our present living trust in God. Careful and constant reading of Scripture increases and emphasizes the necessity of this trust in God and trust in the means He has provided for us to know His will and His love.

This has been the teaching of the Church from the very beginning when there was no New Testament; it is the teaching of the Church today when the New Testament has been appropriated and lacerated by countless unauthorized partizans of interpretations never sponsored by the Holy Spirit; it will be the teaching of the Church until the end of time — because it is the teaching placed in the custody of His Teaching Authority by Christ Himself. And so there can be no other way by which Christ's Revelation can be known to us and handed on by us to those who are to come after us.

It would be hard to find words to present this idea more aptly or more concisely than has already been done by the Fathers of the Second Vatican Council. In the Dogmatic Constitution on Divine Revelation at the end of Chapter II, on the transmission of Divine Revelation, there is the following paragraph:

> "It is clear, therefore, that sacred tradition, sacred Scripture, and the Teaching Authority of the Church, in accord with God's most wise design, are so linked and joined together that one cannot stand without the others, and that all together and each in its own way under the action of the one Holy Spirit contribute effectively to the salvation of souls." (Doc. p. 118).

All this seems so obvious and so logical and so consistent with God's loving care of those who believe, that it is almost impossible for us to understand why it should be so opaque to all of those who refuse belief and stake their salvation on their own interpretation of the Bible and Tradition. Yet, when all is said and done, it is entirely consistent with God's method of dealing with fallen man from the very beginning of the human race until now.

The reason it seems so obvious to us is a product of that great precious mystery — God's Grace. The price of Grace is submissive trust in God. God has furnished that triumvirate of evidence — Tradition, Scripture, and the Teaching Custodian. In the words which I have quoted from Vatican II, "one cannot stand without the others." And even all together they invite but do not compel — and that, too, is exactly as God intends that it should be.

God invites all men and furnishes evidence of His love which He considers sufficient. He who hears the evidence with that submissive trust which God demands will receive the grace to be enlightened by it. As a result of grace all of the items will fall into place and become obvious and the hearer will believe all three and will be furnished with all the tools needed by *menders* as they are intended by God to be used.

Now, the comment that one cannot stand without the others does not mean that the Bible alone is not tremendously consoling tremendously inspiring, and tremendously persuasive to goodness. It is all that and much more. It is an impassioned plea made by utterly convinced witnesses addressed to all mankind and inviting them to come in and share with these witnesses the Bread of Life, which is the Word of God. It does not pretend to be a complete document of revelation. In fact, it is said in so many words that many items of the Deposit of Faith are such that — to use the words of Saint John, "I am unwilling to communicate with thee by ink and pen." (III John 13).

Part of these omissions are prompted by the hostility which surrounded the writers, and part, especially items pertaining to the manner of worship, were omitted because they were always practiced and there was no need to set them down in writing. The weakness of the Bible-only is not that the Bible fails of its purpose, but that its purpose was to invite into the Mystical Body where Christ's mission was continued under Christ's guidance — not to provide a substitute for that guidance.

The nature of the appeal contained in the New Testament is excellently expressed by Father Avery Dulles, S.J. in his precious little essay entitled, *APOLOGETICS AND THE BIBLICAL CHRIST*. These are his words:

> "The testimony of the Apostolic Church, immortally enshrined in the New Testament, is in its way miraculous. A religion so lofty in content, so novel, so unanimous, so self-assured, so effortless, so joyful, so fruitful in good works, so durable in adversity — such a religion, I say, has all the marks of divine revelation. And every other hypothesis proves on examination to be seriously deficient." (p. 40). . . . "The New Testament is not simply a document about Christ. Not even the Gospels are this. They are documents about Christ as the Church sees and reacts to Him, or about the Church as it sees and reacts to Christ. It is the spectacle Christ of addressing His Church, and of the Church responding to Christ which is the great sign of Christian credibility." (p. 43).

The Mystical Body of Christ exercises its mission in accordance with Scripture and Tradition presented by a divinely powered Teaching Authority and clinched to the Sacraments and Sanctifying Grace stemming from them. Its fruit for each of its members is Project Sainthood. Let us be grateful for this gift from God and avoid confusion in the campaign of MENDERS by allowing it to be side-tracked in Bible-only distortion.

We have a treasure which comes to us from God. Without it there is very little to explain our presence in this world. An appalling percentage of those around us, however, are men of good-will who do not have access to our means of Grace because, whether Christian or non-Christian, they have never had the chance to realize the identity between Christ teaching the hearers of the Apostles and Peter — and Christ teaching the hearers of our Bishops and our present Pope. Until we can find the means of encouraging them to carefully examine the evidence that this is true, our dialogue will be largely unintelligible to them.

CHAPTER XV

CHRIST'S PRESENCE FORTIFIES MENDERS FOR DIALOGUE

It is most important that every Catholic should under-stand well the abyss of difference that exists between the Catholic motive for faith-and-behavior and the motive for faith-and-behavior of everyone else with whom he may engage in dialogue. Without this understanding our dialogue is almost sure to lead us very far from the mark.

The reason for this defect in dialogue is that all men of good-will outside the Catholic Church believe that their motive for faith-and-behavior is the same as ours; namely the desire to do the will of God. Not only do they believe that the motive is the same, but most of them believe that the means of knowing the will of God is the same — and that is where the abyss of difference is most dangerous because it can be made to *sound* as if it were quite truly the same.

The Catholic quotes the written word of God and history; the Protestant quotes the written word of God and history; the Jew and the Mohammedan quote the written word of God and history. But, when we come to dialogue, the confu-sion is far worse than mere speaking in different tongues! It is, as it were, speaking the *same* language but having dif-ferent meanings for the words. And this is worse than Babel.

The meanings of the words used by Protestants derive from their individual interpretation of the Bible-only as the word of God. That is the only source of meaning that they know. On the other hand, the meanings of the words used by Catholics derive, not so much from the Bible-only, as from the Source of the Bible — Christ Himself, always present in accordance with His promise made long before any of the New Testament was written. We know of this continuing presence of Christ only because we know that He promised it, and we know that He is God and therefore His promise cannot fail. His presence comes to us, too, in exactly the *way* He promised it, a mystical prolongation of His natural life on earth, but a very real tangible one as well.

The continuity of Christ's presence in His Mystical Body is far different from what Cardinal Newman called a "brick-and-mortar" continuity. It is, however, just as real and just as tangible, in the persons of those who are at any moment the members of His Mystical Body activated by the Spirit of Christ dwelling in them and informed by the Teaching Authority given custody of Christ's word and present in His Vicar, the Holy Father, and the Bishops who are not disloyal to him.

This Teaching Authority *wrote* the New Testament. It has always preserved it and used it as a precious accessory, authored by God Himself through inspiration, to help them to act as the living, breathing, thinking, source of the Word of God to men.

On the other hand, again, those who limit themselves to the Bible-only as the sole source of our knowledge of the Word of God have, for the New Testament, between four and five thousand hand-written documents all of which are copies of copies of copies, re-written for several centuries after their originals were written in the Greek idiom of the first century of the Christian era. Incidentally, these source documents of the New Testament disclose some two hundred thousand variants, most of them, to be sure, unimportant, but the texts themselves giving no clue beyond the admittedly educated guess of the twentieth century scholar. Regardless of education, however, these scholars often cancel each other by widely differing interpretations of the truths revealed by God. Is it too much to say that, aside from joint Scripture research, dialogue with them as to the *meaning* of the word of God can be somewhat worse than useless?

We also treat the Bible as the Word of God, but our faith-and-behavior are motivated by a very different concept of the Word of God from that derived from our individual interpretation of the Bible-only or the Bible and the Torah or Koran and secular history. We, moreover, have reason to know that the Word of God is a very much more intimate source of present belief and behavior than can be found in any book or combination of books.

Unless a non-Catholic is willing to consider all the reasons for this intimacy of our knowledge, our dialogue with him is confused by different meanings for the words. Until he is willing to take a prolonged look at the Catholic motive for faith with the help of an experienced guide, the non-Catholic is usually unaware of the difference.

True, the informed Protestant believes that the Catholic is equally obliged to consider the Protestant's objections to this proposal. There is, however, an objective difference of status between these two points of view. The Catholic motive for faith stems from evidence which purports to come from almighty God and to have been declared by Him to be sufficient for credibility. Until this has been examined and rejected by the Protestant, he cannot justly say that the Catholic has an equal obligation to examine his personal refusal to believe.

The Catholic believes that he can learn to know the will of God and the Word of God from God Himself present in His Church until the end of time. Very many Catholics, however, by their words and acts, do more to obscure this belief than to show it forth. The Devil uses the example of these rebels to promote distortion of this Deposit of Truth, and cripple dialogue before it even begins.

This ferment of dissent within the Church is not a crisis of authority, but a crisis in faith. Those of weak faith are posing as reformers and cheating themselves as well as those within and without the Fold of Christ.

It follows, then, that before our dialogue can possibly be effective, it must be purged of this dross which poses as Catholic belief and behavior but is in truth very far from it. And I repeat again that if every Catholic lived his faith right up to the hilt, the world would be Catholic in one generation. God's revelation of truth and declaration of moral law cannot change since it is the means of salvation provided by God who is perfect and cannot change. Our understanding of it, however, can always be made more secure in the manner made possible by our present access to the Word of God.

It is to try to promote this greater security in the bosom of our Catholic family as preparation for a better presentation of our dialogue of word and example that I have chosen as the title for this chapter: *CHRIST'S PRESENCE FORTIFIES MENDERS FOR DIALOGUE.* I hope to show the intimacy of God's contact with those who accept His way of presenting it.

As the children of Israel were nearing the end of their forty years of probation in the desert, God gave Moses these words of admonition:

> **"Do not forget the long journeying by which, for forty years, the Lord thy God led thee through the desert, testing thee by hard discipline, to know the dispositions of thy heart, whether thou wouldst keep His commandments or not. He disciplined thee with hunger, and then sent down manna, food unknown to thee and to thy Fathers; He would teach thee that man cannot live by bread alone but by every word that proceedeth from the mouth of God." (Deut. 8:2-3).**

This is God's perennial pattern for Project Sainthood from the beginning until the present day. What do I mean by that statement? I mean that God has never left us alone to try to fathom His dealings with us from a written formula. Instead, He has always surrounded us with an ocean of His Providence guiding us intimately and testing our humility, our willingness to trust Him, our willingness to enter in and follow His pattern for Project Sainthood for *Menders*.

God gave our first Parents His direct guidance; He gave the Jews Moses and the Prophets; He has given us His Son and our Church so that we may in truth live, "not by bread

alone, but that we may find life in every word that pro-
ceedeth from the mouth of God." That is what constitutes
Project Sainthood for *Menders* today and it is our privilege
and our bounden duty to try to help the rest of the world
to see it in its true light.

The difficulty of bridging what we have called this abyss
of difference is immeasurably increased by the turmoil
within the Teaching Church. Many legitimate changes have
been made during the present decade with the idea of found-
ing such a bridge, but like a flock of mad hornets, there
have been rebels within who have defied the Teaching
Authority and proposed all sorts of distortions of established
truth that have given the impression to those outside the
Church that the promises of Christ have been denied. This
controversial rebellion from within has reached a point
where some scholars have found in it a hint of the great
apostasy prophesied in the Apocalypse of Saint John.

Even though some of the turmoil is not definite rebellion,
there is very much of it that is almost equally damaging for
a healthy approach to dialogue in that it is constantly debat-
ing and offering opposition to the past and present teaching
of our Popes. Such rebellion and such debate, far from
improving the ground for dialogue, is doing much to injure
the faith of millions of Catholics and giving point to the
warning of Christ which I quoted in the previous chapter:
"When the Son of Man comes, will He find faith on the
earth? "

Most damaging of all, perhaps, has been the combination of
disobedience and debate with reference to artificial birth-con-
trol. This has been aggravated to a degree that has caused the
Holy Father an agony of heart. Another example of this restive failure to be submissive to the guidance of the Holy Father was contained in the very announcement of his thirteen-
thousand world encyclical establishing the permanence of clerical celibacy in the Latin Church. The same headline reported
that the Advisory Board of the National Association of Pas-
toral Renewal "Accepting fully the re-assertion of the law of
celibacy, announce research into newer approaches to the
problem and work for a re-consideration of the law on celi-

bacy aimed at promoting optional celibacy. In other words, aimed at denying the acceptance which they affirm. Is it any wonder that the *SOUTHERN CROSS*, diocesan paper of the Diocese of San Diego, California, reports the Holy Father as commenting: "Sometimes I feel that I am talking to the wind!"

Now, the purpose of ecumenism and the purpose of dialogue is to seek to find ways to invite all men to realize that Project Sainthood is the principal reason for their existence in this world and that God has provided and made known the means of achieving Project Sainthood. But God's way of making it known involves this very abyss of difference we have been discussing. The tendency of the recent attempts at dialogue, all too often inspired by rebels from within, has been to set aside and ignore this basic obstacle.

The result has been a stalemate aptly characterized by one prominent non-Catholic theologian who quite definitely stated his objection to a consideration of the guidance furnished by "Christ present in His Vicar, the Holy Father." His objection, he said, was based on his "own understanding of how God works through men" and "Taking Scripture as his doctrinal norm." In other words, he denied infallibility, not on the basis of the evidence that God has allowed to be available, but on his own understanding of how God works through men with the Bible-only as his reference.

I wrote to this theologian presenting the Catholic viewpoint and asked for his comment. His reply was most gracious and expressive of good-will but emphasized the impasse between the two concepts of the source of the Word of God. A couple of his paragraphs will make this clear:

> "I wish that a clearer distinction could be made between **ecumenism** and **conversion**. Your letter implies that ecumenism, from the Catholic perspective, is mainly a stepping stone toward the conversion of the non-Catholic. I realize that many Catholics hold this position, but it seems to me that the Vatican Council Decree on Ecumenism carefully distinguishes between the two and that, from a point of view of Protestant ecumenical involvement, the distinction is a crucial one."

> "My own feeling is that the ecumenical encounter between Catholics and Protestants must lead each group to ap-

> proach the other in honesty and openness, realizing that
> both groups, and not just one of them, will be trans-
> formed by the encounter.

My reply elaborated his comment on ecumenism and conversion. I wrote:

> "There should, indeed, be a clearer distinction between ecu-
> menism and conversion. The point is this: No one who is
> able to do any sound thinking would become a Catholic
> or remain a Catholic unless he believed that the Catholic
> Church, with all the faults that human frailty has inflicted
> on her, is still the divinely appointed and divinely pro-
> tected Custodian of the Deposit of Truth brought among
> men by Jesus Christ, who is God. This custodianship has
> been guaranteed by Christ until the end of time against
> usurpation or change. In other words, the Deposit of
> Truth is a God-contrived system of belief and behavior,
> specified by Him as the means He has chosen to people
> heaven, and fortified by Him with grace-giving Sacraments
> to make it function. This much cannot be variable.

> "The setting, however, in which this God-given means of
> salvation is offered to men, can and must be kept abreast
> of the changing environment in which men live. God, in
> His Wisdom, has provided the constancy of the former by
> infallible negation of any change, addition, or subtraction
> which the vagaries of fallen man might suggest and have
> suggested throughout the life of the Church. This is the
> one thing which, for two thousand years, has kept the
> Church from descending into the welter of disunity and
> chaos. Without it, unity and continuity are impossible.
> Without it, we and you too, we believe, have nothing."

> "The hope, then, of ecumenism is that God will give grace
> to all men of good-will to see the necessity of this source
> of unity and also to see that it is God-provided. To that
> extent, furthermore, conversion is indispensable for re-
> union. But Pope John and Pope Paul and the Decree on
> Ecumenism all insist that the setting can and must be
> adjusted so that men of good-will can see the necessity of
> the essentials without which none of us have anything
> worth preserving It can be done if it is God's will. If it is
> not God's will, 'we of all men are most pitiable.' " (I. Cor.
> 15:19).

> "It is indeed true that Catholics and Protestants must ap-
> proach each other in honesty and openness, realizing that
> both groups, and not just one of them, will be trans-
> formed by the encounter. And that remains true even
> though there is a divinely guaranteed Deposit of Truth."

This exchange of views in correspondence does explain the situation fairly accurately but does not provide a modus operandi to bring about the desired result. It does, however, provide a suggestion as to how Catholic MENDERS should proceed to prepare themselves to enter into dialogue in a manner that will give some hope of success. First, it must be admitted that the former notion of unconditional conversion to the Catholic Church "as is", forming the sole aim of a Catholic Ecumenism, has the nature of an ultimatum which contradicts the very meaning of dialogue or union. On the other hand, unless the Catholic claim of divinely protected custodianship of the Revelation and the Sacraments brought to man by Jesus Christ, can be supported by evidence deserving acceptance today, the Catholic Church has nothing to offer to anyone within or without the Fold.

Our dialogue should concentrate on the examination of the extent to which this Catholic claim can be made understandable and acceptable to Christians who are not now members of the Catholic Church. The first approach should perhaps be to suggest that history has made it obvious that unity of faith is impossible without divine protection, and since divine protection can be shown to have been divinely promised, some form of it must be discoverable in the world today.

If this much is admitted, it gives a potent invitation to investigate the extent to which the present status of the Church and her past history can demonstrate that custodianship. But when we speak of the present status of the Church, we immediately collide with that obstacle to dialogue – the "as is" mentioned above – which stands in the way of conversion.

And so we should see and be able to explain to others that it is the renovation of the "as is" without damaging the custodianship of the Deposit of Truth that has been the whole purpose of Pope John's quest for renewal and the aim of the Second Vatican Council. The "as is" is the setting in which rests the indispensable prolongation of Christ's teaching of the worship, the truth, the Sacraments and the behavior required by God for salvation and infallibly guaranteed by Him. Without conversion to the latter, the Catholic Church has nothing to offer to anyone.

The setting, however, in which it is offered to the men of the twentieth century has been torn and distorted and is very much in need of renewal before those outside can be expected to see the luster of the jewel. The work and words of Pope John and Pope Paul and the Council have all been aimed at a renewal of the setting so as to clear all the remnants of antagonism generated by centuries of hostile defense on the part of the Magisterium of the Church and the hostile offense on the part of those who had separated themselves from the Church and hostile reluctance on the part of others to be docile to the limitations admittedly involved in the pattern of life prescribed by the God-Man who founded the Church.

It has been the aim of true ecumenism to remove this hostility from within and from without to give clear vision of the necessary inner core of the God-promised and God-centered structure of the Church. The impasse which exists today stems from the disobedience and rebellion, both lay and clerical, which has sought to sabotage the necessary core and most especially to discredit the all-important-God-provided guarantee of indefectibility inherent in the primacy and infallibility of the Holy Father.

The only rescue from chaos lies with those of the clergy and the laity who will stand out from the rebels and live their faith with courage and loyal obedience to the will of Christ as made known to them by the Vicar whom Christ has chosen to represent Him. God will not intervene until the end. The behavior of each one of us during the next few years will have important-bearing on the final answer. Each one of us would do well to ask himself: What should be my part as a MENDER OF THE MESS?

CHAPTER XVI

MENDERS NEEDED IN PERILOUS TIMES

The "team" of books which I have prepared to invite *Menders* to aid our Holy Father to perfect our Church, has been built around the motto: *The Way of Perfection for All, and Project Sainthood for Each*. This motto has, of course, a certain basic perennial application to every Christian and to every individual Catholic. But, in these years following the sessions of the Second Vatican Council, it has lent itself to the consideration of many special problems of great importance to every individual member of the Fold and especially to those who have an urge to *mend* the peril that exists.

The decrees of the Council present a magnificent program of stability and expansion of the influence of the Catholic Church and furnish a pattern upon which *"Project Sainthood for Each"* can be guaranteed. But there is broadcast in the world, and very much more publicized than the decrees of the Council, a poison which, if met only by marking time, might easily drive our individual Project Sainthood into spiritual disaster. These are indeed perilous days and months which await the final implementation and application of the work of the Council and it is my wish to try to help you to see the peril and find the remedy.

It is easy for us to see that these times are *physically* perilous. It is because men, with all their technical knowledge and skills, seem utterly helpless to meet the urgent and oft-repeated plea of all our modern Popes and voiced by our Holy Father, Pope Paul VI: "May the day come on which the discords among people will be resolved, not with the force of arms but rather in the light of reasonable negotiations; and let every war and guerrilla operation give way to constructive collaboration which is mutual and fraternal." He made the same plea, even more forcefully before the meeting of the United Nations in New York. The same plea was voiced before and during World War One and World War Two, and still the same menace makes these times even more perilous physically because of the unbelievable multiplication of the destructive power of the tools of war.

But a peril far more deadly than any physical peril stems from the fact that "Satan is working frantically and using every possible angle and every possible tool to try to poison souls with doubt as to the absolute adequacy of God's present management of His world and His Church." The menace of this peril is aggravated by the utter disobedience of all too many of the clergy and even some of the hierarchy who, contrary to the command of the Holy Father to refrain from unauthorized debate regarding faith or morals, have made themselves prominent by loudly declaring premature opinions upon debated subjects and in many cases doing untold harm to souls by propagating heresy and revolt.

Saint Paul, in his second letter to Saint Timothy, gave him a warning which might well have envisioned the last quarter of the twentieth century:

> "Know this, that in the last days there shall be perilous times. Men will be in love with self, boastful, proud, without scruple, without love, without peace; full of vain conceit, thinking more of their pleasures than of God. They will preserve all outward form of religion, although they have long been strangers to its meaning. ... The men I speak of set themselves up in rivalry against the truth. Men whose faith is counterfeit." (cf. II. Tim. 3:1-8).

The great Apostle may have had in mind a situation to be expected within the lifetime of Saint Timothy himself, but the peril and its sources have been repeated at intervals throughout the life of the Church and certainly they apply to the present day in a sense as grave as any situation that has developed in the entire history of the Church, not excluding the great Arian heresy or the Eastern Schism or the revolt of Luther, Calvin and Henry VIII of England.

The following paragraph taken from the story of Magdalen of Canossa has reference to conditions in Italy at the beginning of the nineteenth century:

> "The times she lived in were indeed sad for the faith. The spiritual and also the moral picture of Verona, like that of other Italian cities at the beginning of the nineteenth century, was altogether distressing. Morals were corrupt, disbelief was spreading, and, in some classes of society, Christian life was at an extremely low ebb. (Casetta, The Servant of God, p. 143). Ignorance of the faith was becoming more widespread because of the campaign of impious and atheistic propaganda. This was being conducted on an alarming scale, and it was leading many people to be uncertain in their faith, while reducing others to a state of religious indifference." (p. 193).

The same could be written of almost any city in North America today.

The nature of the peril is the same now as it was in those times and its gravity has caused Pope Paul VI to express his anxiety in no uncertain terms when he said that one of his "deepest trials" stems from the unfaithful Catholics who "are forgetful of the nobility and gravity of the duties that bind them as Christians and members of the Church.

It is this open and widespread contradiction of the Teaching Authority of the Church which is insinuated or explicitly shouted, even in the Catholic Press, that can certainly be compared with the situation foretold by Saint Paul in his words to Saint Timothy quoted above.

Please to not misunderstand my objective. I have no wish to frighten you by calling these "perilous times." Fear is not the remedy which these times demand for the individual welfare of souls or for those willing to be *Menders*. Every individual Christian should, however, be fortified with sober understanding of the nature and gravity of the situation which justifies the designation of these days as perilous times. The chief and most deadly reason is that the disobedience and contradiction and revolt is coming from within and from sources that, in many cases, possess the most stable appearance of orthodoxy and dependability and official status.

It is for that very reason that it is a deadly peril to those who are inclined to be restive under the restraint imposed by the law of God and the dominion He has a right to exercise over His creatures. It is true that the pressure of hostility voiced by outsiders to some of the doctrines of the Church, arouse some temptation to doubt on the part of the faithful, but the harm to souls from that hostility is as nothing were it not given weight by the ridicule and and contradiction and denial that is being voiced by priests and influential laymen within the Fold.

I am in no sense a "Traditionalist", as that term is now used. Neither am I a Reactionist against the marvelous work of the Second Vatican Council. But, being a convert from ardent Protestantism, it is my duty to vehemently deny the specious arguments of those who are now trying to push me and my co-religionists back into Protestantism and, as our Holy Father of happy memory, Pope Pius XII, has so vehemently warned us, to achieve reunion at the cost of the destruction of Christianity.

And let me emphasize immediately that the Council itself was by no means the source of this peril, even though hot debate may have accompanied its sessions. The Council was, in fact, the *place* for debate in order that the truth might be more clearly defined. A Council is the instrument of God's Church. And God has given us this Church as the Rock of Ages, all-sufficient to bring us to Him as a people and as individuals. The Church gives us sure access to God and to His Word and to His Law and to His Love. It is given to us by God for our salvation and through its Sacraments it is the only means of our salvation.

The Church stands as our protection against Satan who is furiously fighting always to steal souls from God as individuals or as members of groups who rebel. We know, upon God's word, that the Gates of Hell will not prevail against His Church, but that is no guarantee to us as individuals

unless we are docile to the means of salvation and the Word
of God which the Church brings to us.

And how does the Church bring us this Word of God?
He Himself has guaranteed the answer to this question. The
whole New Testament is saturated with it; not as distorted
and torn to bits by individual human testimony, but as presented to the People of God by the Holy Spirit and supernaturally protected from deception by the power given to
Peter, the only one individually promised to us by God as
our sure supernaturally protected guide. And this means that
the Holy Father, aided by the Council, is our guide and
teacher protected by God from day to day against leading us
into error.

And it is the pressure of error, humanly and selfishly
urged, that tends to obscure and delay and separate us from
this supernatural guarantee. The day-to-day teaching of the
Holy Father is protected by God for us as well as his solemn
pronouncements. In fact, the greatest source of the peril of
these times is the widespread publication of opinions contra-
dicting the express teachings of the popes and based on the
utterly false notion that Catholics have no obligation of
obedience to the teaching of the Holy Father except in
matters which are called "*de fide*" because they have been
solemnly declared by the "Chair of Peter", that is, as it is
called "*ex cathedra*".

The truth is that all Catholics have an obligation to be
guided by the encyclicals and allocutions of the popes even
through their wording is technically not irreformable. This
lack of "*de fide*" status, however, only means that a theologian who has reason to question an item of the Holy
Father's teaching has the privilege or perhaps the duty of
submitting the matter to the Holy See and being prepared to
accept the decision with docile obedience. It does *not* mean
that they are subject to open contradiction.

Unless this doctrine is valid, our Magisterium is no better
than the reasoned conclusions of any informed individual or
any group of dissenters. But, this is exactly what God has
promised to His Catholic Church and it may be said that it
is the only valid reason why anyone should belong to it.

To show you, then, how far the modern trend has departed from this stronghold of faith, I wish to comment on two examples which are characteristic of two types of attack from within which contribute to our peril.

The first, which I can only characterize as ecclesiastical connivance in propagating revolt against the infallible Magisterium of the Church, refers to two books reviewed and recommended by a "Catholic" publisher for distribution among Catholics.

The title of the first book recommended displays admirably its nature. It is: *CONTRACEPTION AND HOLINESS, THE CATHOLIC PREDICAMENT*. Except in a false distortion of the meaning of the word "contraception", it can have no connotation other than that of mortal sin. To link it in a title which implies an equation to holiness is a trick of evil which could only be conceived in malice. And this is confirmed in the remainder of the title which can have no other implication than that the contradiction between contraception and holiness is a notion confined to the teaching invention of the Catholic Church and not a part of the positive law of God which binds *all* men and which is declared with regard to Onan in the thirty-eighth chapter of the Book of Genesis, more than a thousand years before there *was* a Catholic Church.

Furthermore, this contradictory notion is supported by the same agents with the claim that the quotation from Genesis has the possibility of an interpretation that the detestable deed for which Oanan was destroyed by God was not the frustration of the act of procreation, but of refraining from taking his brother's widow to wife. And this in the face of the equally clear declaration in the twenty-fifth chapter of the Book of Deuteronomy that the penalty for refusing to take a brother's widow to wife was a mere public rebuke which permitted the scorned widow to take off the culprit's shoe and spit in his face — perhaps humiliation, but very different from being struck dead by God for a detestable deed. It is to be noted also that this contention is put forward in contradiction to the teaching of Pope Pius XI who quoted the passage with reference to Onan as scriptural proof of this law of God which is written in men's hearts. (Casti Connubii p. 20).

The whole sorry business is well characterized in one of the letters addressed to the Editor in protest, as follows: "It fits into the prevailing spirit of insurrection that a supposedly Catholic publishing house regarded as permissible to publish, without imprimatur, a book attacking the basic tenets of Catholic morality, thereby creating a situation where a morally subversive book, is projected into the Catholic masses whose secularized members will eagerly take up its message so appealing to lower nature."

These comments, however, did not deter the editors from printing a review of a book entitled: *OBJECTIONS TO ROMAN CATHOLICISM*, with the effrontery to add the comment: "To have attempted to produce this book with the Catholic imprimatur would, of course, have been absurd." And to bring revolt into the open, the book department offers to sell this book to the Catholic public. One letter discussing this evil complicity gives the following rather hopeless comment: "The subject can hardly be dealt with by ordinary "law enforcement" of the Church because, due to the prevailing ecclesiastical revolution, the number of the law breakers makes it unmanageable." Does not this justify the designation of these as perilous times?

My second example exhibits a widely different type of revolt from within. It may, however, be even more insidious in the end because of its expression of solicitous loyal desire to help the Holy See to understand how to correct its failure to meet the needs of the Church in the Modern World. Indeed, it is not unlikely that the author really believes that too much dependence upon the supernatural protection of the Holy Spirit is part of the antiquated mythology which he calls "non-historical orthodoxy" and which he says is blocking the progress of the Church in meeting these needs.

Perhaps you have read *THE OPEN CHURCH* by Michael Novak. Mr. Novak is undoubtedly a sincere well-meaning Catholic layman who has studied deeply the subject he is discussing and who reports in an arresting way the doings of the Second Vatican Council. He, however, after thoroughly indentifying himself as a layman and an expert newsman, proceeds, without establishing the slightest evidence of qualification, to instruct the Holy Father, the Bishops of the world and the expert theologians of the world in terms of modern thought which, unfortunately, glorying as it does in what he calls "*The Concrete*", is grossly and dangerously misleading.

It is misleading because its notion of the concrete proudly detaches it from one essential guarantee from God without which the Church would be precisely the overgrown, groping, semi-helpless giant pictured by Mr. Novak and all of the adherents of situational ethics, existentialism, humanism, and realism with unfeigned superiority and sophistication. All of their claims are unassailable *except* that Jesus Christ, who is God, has given eminent proof down the centuries that He meant it when He said: "Behold, I am with you throughout all days even until the consummation of the world." (Matt. 28:20).

Mr. Novak and most of his fellow-critics analyze the doings of the Church and the Council with skillful application of the present highly developed scientific knowledge of the human intellect with its "drive to understand" and its "insight", and arrive at a modern synthesis of the religious output of these precious qualities of the intellect which they call the present Church in the *concrete*, living in history and forever groping its way amidst the sinful and stiff-necked men who form its membership. This, incidentally, is precisely what the Protestant Church claims to be.

The danger of this presentation is obscured by the disarming and partially accurate paragraph with which this section of the book is concluded:

> "In short, the abstract concept of a perfect Church, full of truth, never changing, may give comfort to those who need creatures of the imagination to comfort them; it does not exist in the concrete world of history. In the concrete world, God lives and acts in the Church through limited and stiff-necked men, with His unchanging graciousness. God is perfect, full of truth, never changing, but the band of His servants is not."

The last two sentences of this paragraph are indeed well-phrased and accurate and have been taught precisely by the Church for two thousand years. The first sentence, however, is in the context of what has preceeded and is utterly detached from the admission that the perfect, truthful, unchanging God *is* functioning throughout all time in accordance with His promise.

This paragraph which I have quoted comes at the conclusion of three so-called "abstractions" of Novak's "non-historical orthodoxy" which, he says, have no true referents in the concrete world. These three abstractions he cites as follows: That the Church is sinless; that the Church never changes essentially; and that it possesses the whole truth.

The first is, of course, a "straw man" which no one has ever claimed, in the sense that Novak presents it. It is, therefore, quite easily demolished as a substitute for the really precious abstraction that the Church is "holy". Detached from Christ, the Church is, of course, like every other human institution, composed of members only a few of whom are truly holy, all of whom are subject to change, and are frail receptacles of unchanging truth.

But the Church is *not* detached from Christ, and never will be! The tragic flaw in all this frantic effort to open the Church to a demolition of her discipline and doctrine is the utter oblivion of the notion that the *supernatural*, while invisible, is definitely *concrete*. This oblivion is explicitly admitted by Mr. Novak as to his straw-man sinlessness. He says: "What, then, is this "Church" that is sinless? It exists nowhere but in the abstracting mind. *Under a Certain aspect*, namely, the life of God which it shares, the Church is sinless. But the Church is concrete." Indeed the Church *is* concrete, and were it not for the most truly concrete life of God which she *exhibits*, she would long since have ceased to possess the marks of holiness, indefectibility, and infallibility without which she is nothing, but precisely because of which she will emerge from the storm of modern so-called realistic attack, renewed and ever more richly endowed with power to protect her children with the knowledge that they are utterly safe in the hands of Jesus Christ Whose Presence is concrete as nothing else is concrete and who can still repeat His assurance that: "Before Abraham was made, I am." (John 8:58).

Unless the Catholic Church, in the concrete, is holy, indefectible, infallible, and the source of all truth, it is nothing, or far worse than nothing, and, as Saint Paul long ago proclaimed: "We (who seek salvation through her) are of all men most pitiable. (I. Cor. 15:9). But, just as she has demonstrated to an almost unbelievable degree through twenty centuries and twenty-one Councils, she *has* these priceless and indispensable qualities in her solely because she has the Holy Spirit of Christ, in the concrete, in her and in the souls of those who use the Sacraments which He has given her to keep them from sin.

This *is* the essence of the Church and it has been assailed from the very beginning by the "Gates of Hell" with the very same taunt of unrealism and "pie-in-the-sky" credulity. That is as God has obviously intended that it should be. He, of all existence, is *the* Reality and those who trust in Him will never be confounded, but no man will ever be compelled to believe. We who *do* believe, however, can easily see that these are perilous times for those whose faith is fragile or who are weighed down with unrepented sin. But our knowledge of the nature of the peril should fortify us to carry on in Project Sainthood to *Mend the Mess* with serene assurance that howsoever menacing they may be, the Gates of Hell never will prevail — not even in those "last days."

CHAPTER XVII

THE END AND THE BEGINNING

In this farewell chapter, I want to gather together a few quotations which will reinforce and clinch the resolution which you and I should have made by now, to abandon all our former plans and schemes and hopes and fears, and to place ourselves utterly and completely in the hands of Christ remembering His own words to guide us:

> **"Everyone therefore, who listens to these words of Mine, and puts them in practice, shall be compared to a wise man who built his house upon the rock; and the rain descended and the floods came, and the winds blew and beat upon that house, and it fell not, for it had been founded upon the rock." (Matt. 7:24-25).**

We can do nothing of ourselves with any hope of success, unless we constantly advert to the fact that our whole desire is to be useful instruments in God's hands, doing not our own will, but the will of Him who said: "He who abides in Me and I in him, he it is who bears much fruit; because apart from Me, you can produce nothing." (John 15:5).

Every time we worry about our work; every time we are anxious about results; every time we are vexed at failure, it is because we have been trying to run things ourselves; we have been showing off our pride; we have been giving credit to ourselves instead of admitting that it is all due to God. All that He asks of us is that we do our best, with perfect assurance, trying only to do His will as a useful instrument that belongs to Him.

Instead of wasting our anxiety in pursuits of our own choosing, we should say with the Psalmist: "The Lord is my light and my salvation; Whom shall I fear? The Lord is the defense of my life: of whom shall I be afraid? (Ps. 26-1).

To make all this easy for us, God Himself will dwell in our souls just as long as we place no obstacle there by departure from His will.

This indwelling of God's Holy Spirit in us is not just something to give us a feeling of poetic satisfaction. It is just as real as the indwelling of our own souls. The only difference is that this reality, like the reality of the Sacramental Presence of Christ in the Eucharist, is not apparent to our senses. It can, however, be apparent to our intellect and so a source of everlasting joy, no matter what may be our daily experience of failure or success.

The first, and perhaps the greatest source of this joy is expressed by Saint Thomas: "If we are always conscious that God is present in us and sees and judges all, we shall never or rarely sin." And Saint Jerome affirms the same: "The remembrance of God's presence banishes all sin." What greater joy can we experience in this world?

This real union with God begins at Baptism when God first comes to dwell in our heart after it is cleansed from the stain of Original Sin. This presence of God remains unchanged throughout life, so long as we do not deliberately break the contact by mortal sin.

Make no mistake. There is no such thing as intensity or degree of reality in this indwelling of the Spirit of Adoption by which we participate as far as it is possible for human nature to participate in the enjoyment of the Divine Nature. God is present or He is not present in the soul of each person who reads these lines, and that depends on one fact only: whether he or she is, or is not in a state of habitual or Sanctifying Grace. Or, to state the reverse: Whether he or she is not, or is, in a state of mortal sin.

But when it comes to the enjoyment of God's presence and to the benefit to be derived from God's presence and

the merit to be earned because of God's presence: then there
is a world of difference which depends upon our cooperation
with the grace which accompanies and is added because of
God's presence. There is a strange thing too, about the tremendous difference there is in the degree or intensity of our
enjoyment of and benefit derived from God's presence. It
stems from the infinity of God: His infinite goodness and
perfection and lovableness. It is the closeness of our union
with Him that measures our enjoyment of Him even though
He is equally there all the time.

And so, when we, through our abandonment to His love,
can knit that union a little closer, we are being rewarded
with a treasure that is infinite, and when we make that
union a little less secure by even a small venial sin, we are
loosening our hold on a treasure that is infinite in value.
And so it follows that we can gain more with less effort by
acts of the will which unite us to God, than we can by any
amount of effort toward any other end in this world. It is
equally true that we can lose more by even a little dis-
courtesy to our Divine Guest than we can gain in a lifetime
of playing for the favor of other human beings.

We cannot possibly over-emphasize the importance and
the objective reality of the power we will derive from this
advertence to God within us. He wishes it to be that way.
"Behold! I stand at the door and knock. If anyone hears
My voice and opens the door, I will come in to him and sup
with him, and he with Me." (Ap. 3:20). The Gospels are full
of His admonitions. He pleads with His wayward creatures to
accept the love that longs to give us Himself. "I will not
leave you orphans: I will come to you . . . and you shall live
in Me, and I in you." (John 14:18). He promises the perfection which He demands of us if we will but make use of His
help: "As We are One: I in them and Thou in Me, that they
may be perfected into one, that the world may know that
Thou lovest them as Thou lovest Me." (John 17:23).

One who is conscious of the eyes of Christ upon his every
thought, has the power to do all that pleases Him and to
hate all that repels Him. Learn to do all that you do before

the eyes of Christ: "I set the Lord always in my sight: For He is at my right hand that I be not moved." (Ps. 15:8).

In other words, God within us, places at our disposal His infinite power to overcome every adversary — provided we do not make the mistake of trusting our own craftiness first. So, let us get used to working with God's indwelling power all the time, adverting to His presence in everything we do. Then we will never be caught off-guard in an emergency. Especially when sudden temptation comes, we will learn to turn to Him and submit to His will every act of our daily lives.

You may ask: "How am I going to learn to do that?" And I will tell you: First of all, begin when there is no emergency to practice devotion to God within you. Try to advert to Him constantly there, resting in your soul as in a tabernacle. Do everything you do with Him looking on, out of your eyes. Whisper little prayers to Him. There is nothing sentimental about that. On the contrary, it is the smartest habit you could possibly cultivate.

You will not succeed one hundred percent at first. Perhaps days will go by when you will suddenly realize that you have hardly adverted to God-within-you a single time. But do not give up! Every time that you remember that you have forgotten, ask God then and there to help you not to forget so often. God loves humility.

Wives with smart husbands and husbands with smart wives can have their own way and do pretty much as they please all the time, by being selfish and petulant. Smart wives with smart husbands can gain one hundred times as much, one hundred times as often, by always letting God-within-you have *His* way. By being selfless and patient.

Catholics have very potent helps in this regard for which they should be grateful and which they should learn to use much more faithfully. I refer to the seven Sacraments which were. given to us by Christ for this very purpose, namely; to tie our hearts and wills to God in every state of life and at every age, from birth to death. Especially, one might almost say, exclusively, for this purpose, have we been given the Sacraments of Penance and the Eucharist. You who are

Catholics should try to learn to advert to God-within-you whenever you receive these Sacraments or make an examination of conscience. This will encourage you to receive these Sacraments often.

If you learn to practice a fervent devotion to God-within-you on these occasions, it will gradually become second-nature to you throughout the day and in all your prayer. Eventually, it will transform your whole life into prayer and blessed union with God.

You who are non-Catholics should cultivate a firm intention to learn to know God's will and to be determined to abandon your will to His. Practice whatever faith you have with all your might. Pray always for grace to know God's will. Do this with a humble submissive spirit. The importance and value of humble prayer for every soul is beyond the possibility of over-emphasis. If what you have read gives you a hint that God's will calls for further inquiry, you need never hesitate to call upon a priest and ask him to help you, even though you may think that your difficulties are insurmountable. All you need is an honest intention to abandon yourself wholly, body and soul into God's hands. God will do the rest, if you will persevere with confidence in Him. Above all, work at it constantly. Do not allow yourself to put it off till some future time — "For it is God who worketh in you both to will and to accomplish according to His good pleasure." (Phil. 2:13).

If you have received any of the Sacraments of the Catholic Church and have become detached from them, remember this: there is *no* circumstance connected with your life in this world which can be compared with even the smallest of the treasures of heaven. If you knew the half of this truth in its reality, you would not let another hour pass until you had cast yourself into God's arms and begged to be reunited to Him who loves you more than you can ever hope to love Him. There is no sin that need bar you. There is no treasure, no position, which could possibly detain you, if you will but face the truth. You are comparing the infinitely good God to refuse. You are comparing a moment of time to eternity.

There is only one solution to your problem that makes sense; that is reunion with God — He is calling you *now*!

In like manner, each one of us has a precious vocation from God, here and now. That vocation is the same for everyone. It is: to be united to Him always. God is always solicitous for your welfare and is able and willing to do more for you than anyone on earth. He is always present and available to help you. He knows before you do and better than you do, the remedy for all the trials that await you. But be sure of this: He will not force Himself on you. It is the one who "hears His voice and opens the door" who will receive the grace that He almost begs us to ask for.

All of you — if you will only open the door of your heart and invite Him to sup with you, the first thing to happen will be that He will give you the grace to appreciate the privilege as well as the responsibility of His call to you for a more holy life. You will feel a tremendous added incentive to guard yourself and to keep your soul in a state of grace and your body a fit tabernacle for your divine Guest who alone is able to keep you free from sin.

If each one of you will make: "Thy will be done," the motto of every thought and word and act; at home, in business and at worship, then you will come to realize the twofold nature of your call from God. Not only will you then have a special call from God to work as God's instrument for the salvation of your own soul and the souls of others — but, by that very fact, you will be called by God in a manner more intimate and more compelling than other people are called — to be a *Saint* — here and now!

Responding to this call does not automatically make you a saint, but it gives you greater helps than other people have and so gives you a greater obligation to try to be a saint!

God, our Creator, is all holy, that is, infinitely perfect. And yet, Christ, Himself God and Man, has given the counsel to all men: "Do you therefore be perfect as your heavenly Father is perfect." (Matt. 5:48). Could anything be a more direct exhortation to each one of us to be satisfied with nothing less than sainthood?

Saint Paul is aiming at this goal when he says: "I have striven in the noble contest, I have finished the course, I have kept the Faith. For the rest there is reserved for me a crown of justice, which the Lord, the just Judge, will award me on that Day: and not only to me, but to all who have loved His appearing." (II Tim. 4:7-8).

There is hardly a page of Saint Paul's writings that does not plead with every one who has ears to hear to take it from him that nothing makes sense in life that is not aimed at personal holiness. One might say that the *necessity* of saint-hood was burned into his soul at the moment of his conversion, with such intensity that it actually physically blinded his human eyes with the splendor and desirability of the divine glory which could be won, with the help of grace, by every human being. From that moment, for the rest of his life, Saint Paul burned with a zeal to impart this knowledge to other men.

With how many of us would Saint Paul be impatient today, as he was with the Galatians for their tepidity in acting on his exhortations: "O, you silly Galatians! Who has bewitched you, before whose eyes Jesus Christ has been depicted nailed to the Cross? ... Are you so foolish? Have you suffered so much for nothing? " (Gal. 3:1 & 3).

Would Saint Paul say the same to us here? "Oh, you silly Christians! Who has bewitched you? You who are invited to share the love of Christ, nailed to the Cross. Are you so foolish? Are you going to let life go by and be satisfied with anything less than sainthood? "

The trouble with most of us is that we are too used to referring to the saints as we might refer to the Egyptians or the Eskimos: distant human beings, but not our kind. The notion that saints are *other people* is not really an expression of humility, but rather, it is a sort of alibi for spiritual half-heartedness.

When Christ said: "Be ye perfect" He was not joking or exaggerating. He was placing upon us a real obligation to use the great virtue of hope, that He will give us the grace "to

will and to do" what it takes to be saints. He had just told
His disciples how to be saints, namely:

> **"But I tell you, love your enemies, bless those who curse
> you, do good to those who hate you and pray for those
> who revile you and for those who persecute you; so that
> you may be children of your Father who is in heaven,
> who causes His sun to rise upon the good and the bad,
> and rains upon the just and the unjust." (Matt. 5:44-46).**

Now, I can hear you mentally say: "Do you do that
Father? " or, "Do you think you are a saint, Father? " And
I will answer you this way: When I first had the notion to
try to become a priest I was fifty-three years old but I knew
that I needed advice; so the first thing I did was to go to see
my Bishop who was ten years younger than I, but very
much wiser in the things of God. And this is what he told
me: "If you want to be a good priest, never forget that you
are making it your business to be a saint."

I never did forget that advice, but perhaps I did not make
much headway. Then, two years later, I went to the Marian
Congress in Ottawa. There, I saw an electric sign in letters
ten feet high and perhaps two hundred feet long, the legend:
Ad Jesum Per Mariam — To Jesus Through Mary.

There were many beautiful sermons preached extolling
the virtues of Mary, but the more I heard, the more I realized that one needs nothing more than that one motto
upon which to base his start on the road to sainthood and
its foundation of devotion to the Mother of God For saint-
liness is, after all, to direct one's life *Ad Jesum* — to become
united with Him, to live according to His will, to remember
Him always present to us, indwelling within one's soul.

Mary is the one member of the human race eminently
qualified to lead us to this sanctity obtained by union with
Christ, first, because she alone was endowed with sanctity
from the moment of her Immaculate Conception, throughout all eternity. But most of all is she qualified because
Christ gave her to us as our Mother to obtain for us all those
graces from her Divine Son needed to unite us to Him in
holiness of life, that is, to make us saints!

And so, from that day to this, I begin and end every day with Saint Aloysius' prayer to Mary which I have also quoted in Chapter Four:

> **"O, Mary, my Mother, I commend to thy blessed faithfulness, to thy safe-keeping, and to the haven of thy loving kindness, my soul and my body, this day and every day, and in my last hour. All my hope and consolation, all my cares and miseries, all my life and my life's end I commit to thee. And by thy merits and most holy intercession do thou direct and order all my doings in accordance with the will of thine only Son. Amen.**

Being a saint, however, is an active, not a passive operation. But this is what grace will do for you: It will bring to your mind on some occasion the thought: "This is the way a saint would handle this particular situation." You, of course, are free to choose it or leave it. If you act on the suggestion of grace, you will find yourself being reminded again and again until you begin to love being led *Ad Jesum Per Mariam*!

It is under the loving care of Our Lady of Fatima that MENDERS are urged to fight, singly or in groups, to make up what is lacking in the treasury of Rosaries to bring about the conversion of the world. God will do it all if we will allow our Mother of Divine Grace to make us instruments of His will! Are we ready to go?